A YOUNG MAN'S COUNTRY

This photograph of the author, surrounded by his office staff, was taken at the time of his departure from Madaripur in November 1937.

A YOUNG MAN'S COUNTRY

Letters of a Subdivisional Officer of the Indian Civil Service

1936 - 1937

W. H. SAUMAREZ SMITH

WITH AN INTRODUCTION BY

PAUL SCOTT

MICHAEL RUSSELL

First published in Great Britain 1977 by
Michael Russell (Publishing) Ltd
The Chantry, Wilton, Salisbury

ISBN 0 85955 051 6
Set in Linotype Granjon
Printed by The Compton Press Ltd
The Old Brewery, Tisbury, Wilts

Dedicated to A. K. M. Hafizuddin

Contents

A map of the Faridpur District will be found on page 8

Acknowledgements

The author wishes to acknowledge help received from the India Office Library, particularly for the use of the 1926 Ordnance Survey map on which Denys Baker's simplified version (on page 8) is based.

Cuddesdon, 1977 W.H.S.S.

Introduction

I first went to India in 1943 on military duty as a national serviceman. I knew nothing much about the country, did not particularly wish to know more, or to go there. I knew but did not like Kipling because as a boy I hated books about animals that talked. When a bit older I appreciated the qualities of some of the 'Barrack-Room Ballads'. I knew there had been a well in a place called Cawnpore and something called a residency in Lucknow and that some English people had died there during the mutiny of 1857. I had read Macaulay on Clive and Macaulay on Hastings and instinctively preferred the latter to the former. I had an aunt whose husband had been an engineer in India, but he was already dead and all that fascinated me about her was that she played the piano quite well and sang outstandingly badly. In my youth Mahatma Gandhi emerged as a name and a face in the newspapers and in a verse of a song sung by Miss Gracie Fields called 'Granny's Little Old Skin Rug'. In other words India for me was either a bit of a bore or good for a laugh.

Going there with me in 1943 were about one hundred other young men who felt much, and knew as little, as I did and hated the place at first chiefly because the food and the climate had a disagreeable effect on the bowels and the temper. We had no sense of having arrived at the splendid and glittering heart of the British Empire. It was June. The wet monsoon had set in. Everything looked dull and felt damp. Of course it was pleasant as a mere cadet to have a servant of one's own but a bit embarrassing. Mine was called Abdul. He struck me as trustworthy but not bright. He was my first Indian, if I may put it that way. My second was my *munshi*, who agreed that I could have done better in regard to a bearer, and successfully taught me, from a book by a Major Willatt, enough Urdu to pass my elementary examination. I am still able to say, in that language, that the women walked through the fields towards the temple, just as people who learned French in the old days can explain that their postillion has been struck by lightning. My *munshi* also taught me to use the polite form of the verbs when speaking to him, which I suppose was his gentle way of insisting on being treated as a gentleman. I have forgotten his name but remember him kindly.

My experience of India is not to be compared with the much longer and sustained experience of the author of this book, but his affection and my affection for the country may be of the same quality and depth. That is the impression I get. Just when I began to feel at home there I do not know. I was in Belgaum and then in the North West Frontier Province, then Lahore, and passed from there down into Bengal not far (as Indian distances go) from the place in which as we learn from these letters he undertook his first subdivisional responsibility – which meant responsibility for the administration of seven to nine hundred square miles of difficult territory and for the welfare of over a million souls, at the age of twenty-five. At roughly the same age all I had responsibility for was a group of one hundred and twenty men.

I say I do not know when I began to feel at home after that initial experience of what today we call culture shock. But I know when I first felt homesick not for England but for India – that was in Malaya towards the end of 1945 which was when I ducked out of a posting that would have kept me in Singapore for the rest of my time out east. I did not want to be in Malaya, but India; and there, in Bihar, is where I saw my time out. We would jeep into Ranchi for a day or get down by train to Calcutta for a weekend, and be very English and lively and drink gin to toast the boat that would take us home.

But something else was happening. Glad as I was presently to be back home in England I realized that India was also my home. It is difficult to describe but I think in a curious way India in those days was every English person's home, even if it had not been visited. Because we ruled it and benefited from it, it contributed to our well-being and upbringing. It was mysteriously in our blood and perhaps still is. In any case, that is what I felt and gradually I became appalled at the thought of how little I knew of our history there. I have been reading that history now for thirty years and have been back several times. But time and again I have closed a book dissatisfied because the book has not told me how it *worked* for ordinary English people doing jobs there. There were never many of them.

Mr. Saumarez Smith was one: a young man with an older man's load on his shoulders. As he himself writes, for the British, India was very much a young man's country. There is no counterpart today. Morally, I know, it was wrong – that young people of one race should exercise executive, administrative and judicial power over people of all ages of another race. But, that apart, the job was there to be done by someone and it has for a long time seemed to me that in this situation there was a moral challenge met rather well by the people who accepted it, as a job of work, and who are in danger of disappearing into the mists of history and anonymity because they have seemed to think that readers would be bored by accounts of what the job was and how it was done, and so have in general preferred to write memoirs of princes and palaces, tiger, duck, viceroys, pro-consuls, punkas, polo and poodle-fakers, temples, monuments; and tell plain tales from the hills: all of which leave an erroneous impression that no young Englishman, or aging Englishman, or his wife, had in mind, in heart, on the conscience, the workaday affairs of the workaday Indian world.

What follow are letters written by a young man to his parents. They tell us a lot about what it was really like to run a subdivision in the late nineteen thirties (when the political pressure was on). They reveal – as they must – a young man's naïvety and prejudices, but then – for me at least – their value is enhanced by the writer's refusal to tamper with them to bring them more into line with what I suppose is called current thinking. It is fascinating of course to compare this straightforward record of what it was to be a *chota sahib* on his way to becoming a *burra sahib* with the caricatures in so much of our fiction and popular history. And I find the extensive notes at the end of each section, written recently, as interesting as the letters which – to me – mostly reveal the qualities that I often look for in vain: the good intentions, the hard slogging, the short dense stolid shadow cast by the ordinary man doing his extraordinary job under an Indian sun.

PAUL SCOTT

I

Background

My father was a methodical man. He kept, in two large box-files and in chronological order, all the letters which I wrote from India to him and my mother between 1934 and 1947, when I was in the Indian Civil Service. When he died in 1950 I took them over, but never really studied them.

My retirement in 1975 gave me additional leisure. I had long realized that, of the period of nearly thirteen years that I worked in India, the sixteen months from July 1936 to October 1937 were the most memorable. That was the time when I held my first responsible appointment, as Subdivisional Officer of Madaripur, in the district of Faridpur in East Bengal. The population of the subdivision was rather more than one million, and I was less than twenty-five years old when I went there. It is true that for the British in India, it was very much a young man's country – though possibly not that young!

A reason why the letters may be of some interest to a wider circle of readers than students of the British Raj is that Madaripur lies in what is now Bangladesh. Nature and man have combined to make Bangladesh one of the most afflicted countries in the world. In the years which have passed since I worked there, the political system has changed out of recognition. The terrain has not. Greater knowledge of the natural conditions in which Bangladeshis live may lead to greater interest; and greater interest to greater sympathy.

During my second year at Cambridge I decided to try for the Civil Service. Entrance to the Indian Civil Service and the administrative grade of the Home Civil Service was by the same examination. In June 1933 I completed my degree course, with a combination of law and mathematics. After a brief but intensive month's course at Davies's, the well-known crammers, I sat for the Civil Service exam at Burlington Gardens. This was rather in the nature of a trial trip, as I was a year too young to get into the Home Civil, which was my main objective, since I had no links whatever with

India. However, I did sufficiently well to qualify for the Indian Service. This posed a dilemma. Should I mark time for a year, and try for the Home Civil again in 1934? I decided to go for the bird in the hand.

Each successful entrant to the I.C.S. was very quickly assigned by the India Office to a particular Province, in which normally he served throughout his career. He was allowed to indicate his preference between the Provinces. When confronted with this problem, I was in a state of almost total ignorance. I consulted the only person whom I knew with the requisite knowledge. Sir William Barton had had a very distinguished career in India. Starting in the I.C.S. in the Punjab, he had moved into the Indian Political Service and ended his years in India by holding in succession two of the most coveted posts, the Residency of Mysore and the Residency of Hyderabad, from which he had retired in 1930. He had married a cousin of my father. I asked his advice. He listed the nine Provinces – Sind and Orissa did not become separate Provinces until 1937 – in order of preference. The Punjab was at the top of the list, and Bengal at the bottom. I replied to the India Office in accordance with Sir William's advice; but I did at least include Bengal in my list, which many of my fellow-entrants did not. I was assigned to Bengal.

There were several reasons for the unpopularity of Bengal – its hothouse climate, its long history of political unrest, the un-martial character of its people. The main cause of its unpopularity at that particular time was the Terrorist Campaign. Beginning with the Chittagong Armoury Raid in April 1930, the next two years saw a large number of assassinations and attempted assassinations; the victims included two District Magistrates, a District Judge, and the Inspector-General of Prisons. The Governor, Sir Stanley Jackson, himself had a narrow escape in February 1932, a month before he handed over charge to Sir John Anderson. During the first four months of Sir John's office, another District Magistrate and a District Superintendent of Police were murdered. By 1933, the situation had improved; but, to use a meteorological phrase, the further outlook was unsettled.*

Entrants to the I.C.S. had to serve a year on probation at Oxford, Cambridge, London or Trinity College, Dublin. During this year they learnt something about Indian history and law; they had to pass a riding test; and they acquired a grounding in the language of their Province. I returned to Trinity College, Cambridge for my probationary year. This was an enjoyable and carefree time. Instructed by an elderly gentleman who had long previously served in the I.C.S. in Bengal, and whose blood had been so

* For this paragraph, I am indebted to *Years of Change in Bengal and Assam* by Sir Robert Reid (Benn, 1966).

thinned that he wore a thick greatcoat in the height of summer, I learnt the rudiments of Bengali. His lessons were supplemented by a Linguaphone record which, through constant repetition, is still engraved on my memory; and by a Phonetics Lecturer in King's with a prominent Adam's apple which moved alarmingly as he demonstrated a Hottentot Click. We were taught riding in some stables off Jesus Lane by one Captain Cooper, whose team of horses had the docility of a circus troupe. He had a sadistic streak, and always allocated the largest beast to the smallest Indian probationer. Our lecturer in Indian Criminal Law was profoundly dull, but the Censor of Fitzwilliam House contrived to arouse an interest in Indian History despite an uninspiring textbook.

In August 1934 we all foregathered in Burlington Gardens again for the passing-out examination. This having been successfully negotiated – in fact I managed to achieve the second place – the next landmark was the signing of a Covenant with the Secretary of State for India on 11 October 1934, which made me a 'Member of the Civil Service of India, in the Presidency of Fort William'.

* * *

A fortnight later I sailed East from Southampton with my sister. She was to be married in Singapore to Ronald Bottrall, the poet, whom she had met in the United States, where they were both Commonwealth Fund Fellows in English, he at Princeton and she at Yale. He had become Professor of English at Raffles College. After giving her away in Singapore Cathedral, I sailed on to Calcutta.

There I learnt that my first appointment would be as an Assistant Magistrate in the district of Rajshahi in North Bengal. It was the practice for new members of the I.C.S. in Bengal to spend their first year as Assistant Magistrates at the headquarters of a district, during which their main objectives were to pass their 'departmental examinations' in language and law, held each May and November; to try simple cases; to learn how a district office was run; to do some touring in the district; and generally to find their feet.

I could write at some length about my experiences in Rajshahi, which were mainly pleasant, thanks largely to a very friendly and affable District Magistrate and his wife. I went through my first hot weather and my first monsoon – the breaking of that monsoon is unforgettable. Sir John Anderson paid a gubernatorial visit to the district. I had one holiday in Darjeeling, and saw Kinchinjunga for the first time; and another in Shillong. As a prelude to an independent charge, however, it must be said that my actual training in administrative and magisterial work was neither rigorous nor arduous.

During their second cold weather, the Assistant Magistrates spent four months in 'Settlement Camp', learning about land revenue matters. This was an extremely valuable – and enjoyable – experience, living under canvas, riding round the villages, and taking part in the elaborate process of a field-by-field survey and recording of the detailed rights of every landlord, tenant, and subtenant. We were working in the north of Dinajpur District, with the peaks of the Eastern Himalayas visible on the distant horizon. During the first part of the Camp we had with us our contemporary juniors in the Indian Police.

I had not passed all my departmental examinations in November 1935, so at the end of my Settlement Training, I had a brief posting as Assistant Commandant of Buxa Detention Camp. This was a Camp for political detainees, young Hindus suspected of terrorist activities. It was situated in the foothills of the Himalayas near the border with Bhutan, a long way from any centre of political activity. My duties were negligible, and I had ample time to prepare for my remaining examinations, which I passed successfully in May.

I have given this brief summary of my entry into the I.C.S. and of my first eighteen months in Bengal in order to set the scene for the letters from Madaripur. It is now necessary to give a few facts about the subdivision of Madaripur and the district of Faridpur in which it is situated.

* * *

Faridpur district lies to the south-west of Dacca, on the opposite side of the Ganges. Averaging the figures for the decennial censuses of 1931 and 1941, the population of the district in 1936 must have been about 2,650,000. (The growth rate in the decade exceeded twenty per cent.) There were four subdivisions in the district, of which Madaripur, in the south-east, was the largest, with a population of 1,150,000. It is, oddly, not easy to state the area of the subdivision: in 1941 it was 961 square miles, but in 1931 it was only 716 square miles, the difference being accounted for by alluvial accretion. The subdivision had only one town (Madaripur itself) and over a thousand villages, the density of population being the remarkably high figure of 1,300 to the square mile.

Figures by themselves do not convey a great deal. It may give a better idea to say that Madaripur compares fairly closely, both in population and size, with Hertfordshire.

Just under three-quarters of the people were Muslims and just over one-quarter were Hindus. Of the Hindus, about one-third were members of the Scheduled Castes, or Untouchables. Only eight per cent of the population were literate, roughly 40,000 Hindus and 40,000 Muslims – so proportionately the Hindus were a great deal more literate than the Muslims. Only 20,000 people altogether were literate in English

For a description of the climate of the district, we may turn to the *Faridpur District Gazetteer*, written by Mr. L. S. S. O'Malley I.C.S., and published in 1925:

> The climate is not characterised by extremes of heat and cold, and the variation of temperature is comparatively small. . . . Mean temperature remains at 83° from April to September and falls to 66° during the cold weather, the mean minimum being lowest in January, when it is 53°. At the same time humidity is great, and many people consequently find the climate relaxing. The air is rarely dry, except in the cold weather; even in March the frequent occurrence of storms produces humidity in the atmosphere. In the rains, when a moisture-laden wind blows from the east or south-east, it is exceedingly damp, but the steadiness and strength of the wind are an alleviation of the damp heat. The average annual rainfall of the district is 73 inches; the heaviest precipitation takes place at Palong (94″). During the monsoon months, June to September, the monthly rainfall is uniform being 13″ to 14½″ per month, except in September when it falls to 9″. In May and October, the months which precede and follow the monsoon, the rainfall is 9″ and 6″ respectively, and is due to the incursion of cyclonic storms, when heavy rain may fall for days together.

In England the course of a river is static. The Thames today flows approximately where it flowed in Saxon times. In Bengal, rivers change their course from year to year. An understanding of this is essential to appreciate the conditions under which the people of the Ganges and Brahmaputra delta live. Let me quote Mr. O'Malley again:

> Since the time of the Permanent Settlement (1793) almost all the rivers have changed their courses to such an extent as to leave dry the beds in which they then flowed. Alluvion and diluvion still proceed, especially in and along the Padma and Meghna,* the channels of which swing from side to side of their sandy beds. The surface of the country in their neighbourhood is thus subject to constant change. Land in their beds and along

* The Padma is an alternative name of the mainstream of the Ganges, after it has been joined by the Brahmaputra; it formed the northern boundary of Faridpur District. The Padma joined the Meghna, which formed the eastern boundary of the district.

their banks is perpetually being cut away and re-formed as the rivers shift their channels, now eroding the land and now building it up. At one place the river cuts into its bank and washes away village sites: at another the shore receives a new deposit of alluvion. Similarly in the river beds themselves islands, called chars or diaras, are thrown up and washed away as the river cuts out new channels for itself. These lands are the subject of perennial disputes, recurring riots and protracted litigation, which is of a complex character, owing to the difficulty of knowing whether the land is an accretion or a reformation *in situ* and to the absence of fixed landmarks, as the rivers every year carry on a continual process of destruction and renewal....

The sequel to the emergence of a fertile char is well described by Mr. J. C. Jack in his *Faridpur Settlement Report* (1911): 'The rivers fall rapidly and rise as rapidly. The new land is often very extensive and the locality of its formation can never from year to year be anticipated. As soon as the river has receded, the land is ripe for cultivation, and if any delay occurs in transplanting into the liquid mud which the river has left, there is great danger that the river will rise again too soon for the crop to be harvested. Even if the whole river had belonged to a single landlord and there were no disputes about title, there would still be disputes between the cultivators of villages contiguous to the new formation and between the cultivators of a single village. The crops which these lands supply are too valuable for everybody not to desire the chance of reaping them; they require no effort, the land needs no ploughing, the crops need no weeding; it is only necessary to transplant when the river has gone and to harvest when the river returns. It is only human nature to make every effort to reap so easy a profit, and the history of these chars is such that that effort will invariably take the direction of turbulence and rioting.'

It was largely in consequence of lawlessness in connection with the chars of this (sc. Faridpur) and the Dacca district that the Bengal Alluvial Lands Act was passed in 1920, with the object of preventing the turbulence and rioting which hitherto had so frequently accompanied the formation of alluvial land.

I have mentioned that the density of the population of the subdivision was 1,300 to the square mile – a very high figure indeed, and varying little throughout the area. The vast majority of the men were cultivators, and the two main crops were paddy and jute. (The harvested grain of paddy is rice, and it is incorrect to use the latter word for the growing crop.) Paddy was the food crop. There were two main varieties: 'aus' or summer paddy, and 'āman', or winter paddy, the principal crop, which was harvested in November/December. Jute was the money crop. It was sown in April and cut in August. It was transported in small country boats to storage centres – Charmugria, the main jute-centre of Madaripur subdivision, features often in the letters – and then shipped to the jute-mills lining the River Hooghly north of Calcutta.

* * *

The letters must speak for themselves. They have been printed exactly as I wrote them forty years ago, with a minimum of editing. In practically every instance where an omitted passage is indicated by '...', the omission relates to comments on items in my parents' letters of purely family interest. My father had been in charge of two country parishes, Waldershare and Coldred, five miles from Dover, since 1921. He was 62 in 1936, and my mother was 58. My sister Margaret (two-and-a-half years older than myself) and I were their only children, so it was a great wrench for them when we both left for the East together. It must be remembered that transcontinental air travel was then in its early days. When I left my parents in October 1934, it was in the expectation that I would not see them again before the spring of 1938 at the earliest. All this may help to explain why I wrote to them with such conscientious regularity even when I had little of much interest to say and very little time for letter-writing; but it must be admitted that two regular airmail services each week were a helpful stimulus, for 'any time is no time'.

I have been sorely tempted to edit or omit some passage of startling naïvety. In extenuation, I must repeat that I was less than twenty-five years old when I went to Madaripur, and less than twenty-six when I left. Style and punctuation also have been left unaltered; I now dislike my practice of writing low numerals in figures rather than words, which occurs in the letters written at leisure as well as those written in haste; I have lost my excessive love of the ampersand; but I have (evidently) retained my love of the semi-colon.

A final word needs to be added about the explanatory notes. These have been compiled mainly from my memory, endorsed by occasional reference to the brief and dull diaries which I used then to keep. Their purpose has been both to supplement certain gaps in the narrative, and to elucidate something of that strange 'world of chaprassies and chaukidars and "144" cases and tadbir and A.G.B.'s objections and D.W.s', to which I referred at the end of my letter of 27 September 1936.

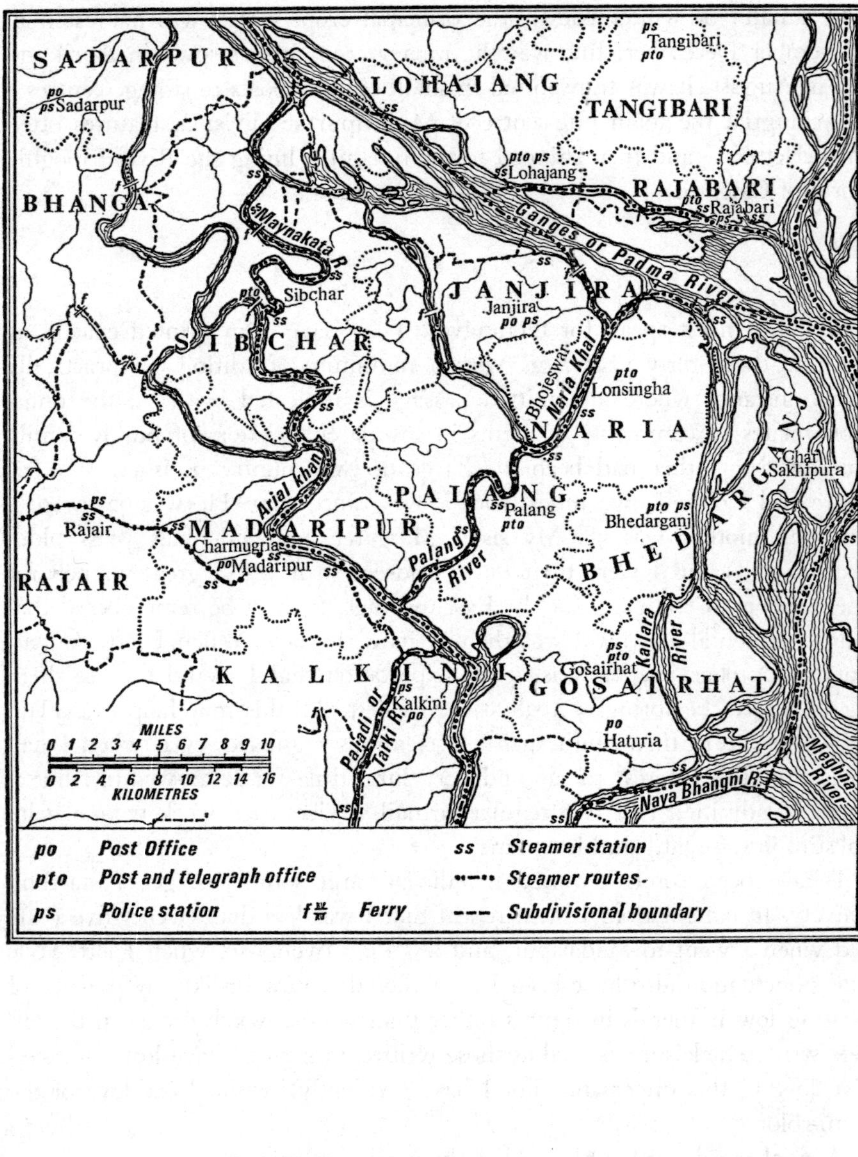

SADARPUR
Sadarpur
LOHAJANG
Lohajang
TANGIBARI
Tangibari
RAJABARI
Rajabari
BHANGA
Maynakata R.
Sibchar
SIBCHAR
JANJIRA
Janjira
Ganges or Padma River
Bhojeswar
Naria Khal
Lonsingha
NARIA
Char Sakhipura
BHEDARGANJ
Bhedarganj
PALANG
Palang
Arial khan
MADARIPUR
Charmugria
Madaripur
Rajair
RAJAIR
Palang River
KALKINI
Kalkini
Paladi or Tarki R.
GOSAIRHAT
Gosairhat
Haturia
Kailara River
Naya Bhangni R.
Meghna River
MILES
0 1 2 3 4 5 6 7 8 9 10
0 2 4 6 8 10 12 14 16
KILOMETRES
po Post Office
pto Post and telegraph office
ps Police station
f Ferry
ss Steamer station
Steamer routes.
Subdivisional boundary

2

Letters

21 June 1936 - 17 October 1936

Rajshahi, North Bengal
21 June 1936

On Monday I heard that I was appointed to have charge of Madaripur subdivision in Faridpur District. On Tuesday I heard that I had passed my Departmentals completely. So this week really marks the end of my 'apprenticeship'. After seven years in which I have had to take nine exams, it is difficult to believe that I have finished my education, in the formal sense of the word. I shall probably be in Madaripur until I come on leave.

My address will be: Subdivisional Officer, Madaripur, District Faridpur, Bengal, India. It may be possible to abbreviate this, but this will serve until I let you know definitely. Telegraphic address, Madaripur Bengal. Looking after any subdivision is a job to take all one's time and ability, and I understand that Madaripur is a particularly important one. I suppose I ought to be flattered, but it's really rather a terrifying prospect. I feel as you, Father, probably felt on your way to your first curacy!

I don't know quite when I shall leave here, but probably before this week is out. I shall spend two or three days in Calcutta en route, chiefly to buy furniture. I hope I may see Mrs. Blank[1] on her way through to Bombay and England, and I may be able to give her a box of unwanted clothes and books to be despatched to Waldershare, as she very kindly offered to take anything home I wanted. I'll be able to let you know further details about this next week.

I've been able to find out a good deal about Madaripur. Hajara, the new District Magistrate, had come from Faridpur, so was able to tell me a certain amount, and I've been in correspondence with the present S.D.O., S.K. Dey.[2] By consulting your map, you'll be able to see that it's in the delta of the Ganges and the Brahmaputra. There is no railway within fifty miles, and no road worthy of the name in the whole subdivision. All communication is done by water. I have the use of a Government launch (called Rosalind)[3] which I share with the Subdivisional Police Officer (S.D.P.O.). M'pur is a big jute-growing centre, and the town has almost exactly the same population as Rajshahi (26,000), but is more congested. The whole of the mofussil is under water at this time of year. It is out of the question to take Peter; even in the cold weather, a horse is no use. I am trying to sell him to one of this year's Assistant Magistrates. Luckily for my pocket, a car is equally impossible

The area of the subdivision is 710 square miles, and the population just under a million, nearly all rural. You can see from this what a densely populated area it is. 70% of the people are Moslems. I hear that my bungalow is quite a nice one, but that my office is all at sixes and sevens, being moved to a temporary site owing to the erosion of the river. There will be several Deputy Magistrates[4] to help me at headquarters, but I shall have my hands kept exceedingly full, not only in Madaripur itself, but in my tours throughout the subdivision. But, given good health, it will do me good to get my teeth into a proper job at last. And I hear that Madaripur is healthier than most of Bengal. My District Magistrate will be one Hill,[5] who's had about 10 years' service, and whom I think I shall like. I shall probably be the only Englishman in M'pur itself, but I believe there are some jute wallahs not far away.

I don't know where my next letter will be written from – probably Calcutta. From now on, my correspondence may become a little scrappy, but I'll do my best to send you some sort of a letter each week. An S.D.O. is liable to be called on suddenly to cope with any emergency – famines, floods, riots – and an irregular life is not conducive to regular letter-writing.

Rajshahi, North Bengal
24 June 1936

I am sending these things home through the very kind agency of Mrs. Blank. I shall never have occasion for a second dinner-jacket suit out here, particularly a heavy-weight one. It can be kept in moth-ball against my return, when it will come in very well for changing for dinner at home.

The books are those I selected as being least likely to be referred to, and at the same time, ones which I did not want to be spoilt by the damp of Bengal.[6] Would you put them all together in my 'Trinity' bookcase. Don't throw away the dust-covers; it's a fad of mine to keep them, and they come in very useful when packing up!

Rajshahi, North Bengal
26 June 1936

I'm leaving here tonight, staying in Calcutta for Saturday and Sunday morning, and arriving in Madaripur on the 29th, Monday. I shan't have a minute to spare in Calcutta, so I'd better dash off a quick letter here and now.

This week has been a pretty full one. At office I had a couple of cases to finish off, and I just managed to deliver the second judgement yesterday. I said good-bye to Peter and his sais yesterday morning, and hope to hear soon that Wooller[7] (Assistant Magistrate, at Jalpaiguri) has approved of him and bought him. Tuesday was a particularly eventful day; it started with the King's Birthday Parade, for which I had to don my ridiculous morning suit for the first time since the Governor's visit nearly a year ago. Then I had a land dispute to settle about 8 miles away. I rode out after breakfast to the scene of action, which was a series of paddy-fields on an island in the Ganges. The river-bed is constantly changing, and every year there is a quarrel about who shall harvest the paddy. The crop was just ripe and ready for cutting, so I made a temporary settlement, and the two lots of tenants can fight the matter out (metaphorically) in court later. It's only too probable that they will fight the matter out literally in the course of harvesting! This is an extremely common type of dispute in alluvial lands. It was noon by the time I'd finished, and the ride back, on the longest day of the year with the sun shining, was pretty hot and tiring.

. . . I've been having a bit of a bother with my servants, as the man I was going to take to Madaripur as cook has got a skin-disease of his hands, which my bearer[8] noticed just in time. However, I've got hold of the old chap who cooked for us last year, and he'll do temporarily at any rate. I'm also taking the young scullion, who's a promising lad; the trouble with him was a stupid old grandfather who'd rather have seen him unemployed than let him leave the district. However, his objection had been overruled! It's very easy here to supplement one's staff at a moment's notice, for the supply greatly exceeds the demand, and a young I.C.S. sahib is a real catch!

. . . I must go to office for the last time now. It has been some job supervising the preparation of 30 pieces of luggage![9]

Madaripur, Dist. Faridpur, Bengal
4 July 1936

I got to Calcutta on Saturday morning, and had a most successful day's shopping. My chief purchases were furniture; I got a drawing-room suite, a dining-room suite, a bookcase and a dressing-table, all in good unornamented teakwood for Rs. 350/- – second-hand, of course, but a really magnificent bargain.[10]

On Sunday I made my Communion at the Cathedral, and after beakfast taxied out to the Oxford Mission, and had a long & helpful talk to Father Douglass.[11] I then lunched with Kitchin,[12] who was also on his way to join a subdivision. After lunch I caught the train here.

It was a comfortable journey; train as far as Khulna, where I changed into a small steamer. This took me direct to Madaripur. I was lucky enough to find a Mr. and Mrs. Boyle on board; he is the Steamer Co. Agent, who lives at Charmugria (just across the river from here, and a big jute-centre), and he is one of the six Europeans in the subdivision.[13] I'm going over to Charmugria on Sunday afternoon to meet the others.

I went straight to the S.D.O.'s bungalow, & found Dey busy winding things up. It's a nice bungalow, large, airy & clean; I'll describe it in detail in a later letter. I found my servants and heavy luggage had arrived safely from Rajshahi. Dey told me a great deal about the subdivision, and it was lucky that we had the inside of two days together. I liked him a lot, and hope we may meet again.

He left on Tuesday afternoon, & since then I have done little but work. This is generally acknowledged to be one of the most important and heaviest subdivisions in the Province. I have to spend 10 or 15 days each month touring in the mofussil. This will provide great variety, & will be rather fun in the launch. I shall usually tour with the Subdivisional Police Officer (S.D.P.O.). He is a nice young Mahommedan called Hafizuddin,[14] & I think we shall get on very well together. (It is vital to the efficiency of the administration that we should).

My daily progamme is: 7-11, confidential work & interviews in my bungalow; I have a most helpful confidential clerk.[15] 11.30-4.30 or 5, office work, the most important being the 'General File.' This is the management of the preliminary stages of criminal cases before they get to the stage of actual taking of evidence – e.g. hearing complaints, and dismissing them as false, or sending them for local enquiry, summoning the accused etc. etc. I shall have practically no time for criminal work myself; the bulk of this is done by my Deputy Magistrates. Actually, I've just taken up an extremely important case, at the request of both parties, an alleged abduction of a Hindu girl by a Moslem; all the people concerned are *bhadra-lok* (gentry) and my successful (or otherwise) handling of the case will probably decide the opinion of the local Bar about my judicial capacity.

After office, I usually have to pay a visit to the Jail,[16] of which I am in charge. There are only about 80 prisoners, mostly people awaiting trial or under trial; those convicted go to Faridpur. Then I frequently have a school committee-meeting or some other meeting. I am president of all the high schools in the subdivision, and this will be an important side of my work.[17] I probably do a little more correspondence before dinner at 8.30. After dinner, I am going to keep free as far as possible, but early to rise means early to bed too.

I'm feeling very fit, and finding life pretty interesting. Next week I start my touring with a visit to Faridpur.

My corespondence will inevitably be a hurried affair, & it's a great bore that to catch the usual Air Mail I have to write on Saturday instead of Sunday. The posts here are appalling.

I shall always seal my letters to you, as there are some pretty funny things going on in this subdivision. Please tell me if you see any sign of the envelope being tampered with.

P.S. Most important, & I nearly forgot all about it. Mrs. Blank is bringing home a case of books for me. She sails in the Cathay, lands in Marseilles, travels across in the Blue Train, and gets to England on July *18th.* Verify the time of her arrival at Dover (or possibly Folkestone?) from Pickfords, and, by hook or crook, meet the boat & take the case. There is a letter inside it.

Madaripur, East Bengal
10 July 1936

I shall be able to write you a decent letter this week, as I am on board a steamer[18] bound for Faridpur, where I am going to attend a District Board Meeting.[19] I am staying with the Collector and his wife, the Hills, and I look forward to meeting them, as he is my 'boss'. The vibrations of the steamer account for the vagaries of my handwriting.

This week has not been quite such a wild rush as the first. The spate of callers has somewhat diminished, I'm beginning to get the hang of the routine work, and I haven't had to take any big criminal cases, which require more time than anything else.

On Sunday I had interviews without a moment's break from 9 till 12. I'm going to post a notice that in future interviews will only be given on Sundays on urgent business & by special arrangement. That afternoon, Hafizuddin and I went over to Charmugria (the big jute-centre two miles away) and had tea with the Boyles. They have a nice garden, and are very friendly people. They are also keen Roman Catholics. After tea, we had a meeting of the Marwari[20] merchants, and extracted a promise of Rs.500/- from them for the King's Memorial Fund. I then returned to M'pur for a Committee Meeting of the Madaripur High School.

I needn't describe my activities from Monday till Thursday in detail. They included visits to the Veterinary Hospital and the Public Library, and Committee meetings of the Girls' School and Co-operative Bank.[21] I know absolutely nothing about Banking, but I have to be ex officio chairman of the Co-op Bank. It really is amazing the way people defer to one's opinions; the other directors are all shrewd business men, mostly over 40; and yet they genuinely welcome a young and inexperienced person like myself to be their chairman. The reason is that they all have an axe to grind, and none of them really trust each other, whereas they know that I am impartial.

As I spend at least two hours every day doing what is called the 'General File', I must try to describe this part of my work. Though I don't do much criminal case-work myself, all cases come to me in their preliminary stages. After a crime is committed, the victim either goes to the police, who take up the investigation & submit a report to me subsequently; or else they complain direct to my court. I hear their complaints; if I think their story is entirely false I can dismiss the case there and then; if I think it is suspicious, I can send the case to a local officer for an enquiry and report; if I think it is true, I can summon the accused. This getting hold of the accused is the next stage; if he doesn't obey the summons, a warrant of arrest is issued. There are nearly always 2 or 3 accused in every case, and it may require several adjournments, before they have all appeared. Once they have all come, the case is adjourned to another date for evidence. When that date comes, I transfer the case to one of my Deputy Magistrates, who does the actual hearing of the witnesses, & passes judgement and sentence. Each adjournment is for a period of about three weeks, so it is usually a couple of months after the original crime before the witnesses are actually examined. A usual day's 'General File' consists of 7 or 8 new complaints, 20 or 25 cases in one or other of the preliminary stages, and 3 or 4 cases for transfer to the Deputy Magistrates. I also usually have one or two petty cases of food adulteration, refusal of vaccination, or plying a boat without a light, in which the accused invariably pleads guilty, and is fined a rupee or so. What I have found is that it is one thing to have passed an examination in the Criminal Procedure Code, and quite another to have the procedure at one's finger-tips, to apply correctly as each new case crops up.

On my return from Faridpur, I am going out on tour for four days in the launch, so next week I shall, if I can find time, be able to tell you something about the other side of my work. My life will be a succession of days spent on tour, followed by frantic bursts of work at headquarters trying to catch up the accumulation of work. There is of course a lot of drudgery routine work and signature-appending. But there is also a great deal of work where the personality of the S.D.O. counts, and where his ability to get other people to follow his lead is tremendously important. So far I've met with much friendliness and little hostility, but it may not always be so easy.

But you'll be wanting to hear about my bungalow. My compound is occupied chiefly by a large tank,[22] full of weeds; I may get it cleared, and use it as a swimming-bath. The garden is very jungly, but I hear that the Deys had a fine show of flowers last cold weather, and I'm getting hold of a gardener as soon as I can. I've come at just the right time of year, as he can tidy the garden up this month and start planting cold weather seeds next month. The Boyles will be able to help me a lot with their experience and advice.

The bungalow is clean and very airy. Except for the drawingroom the rooms are on the small side. Here are plans of the compound and the bungalow [now re-drawn].

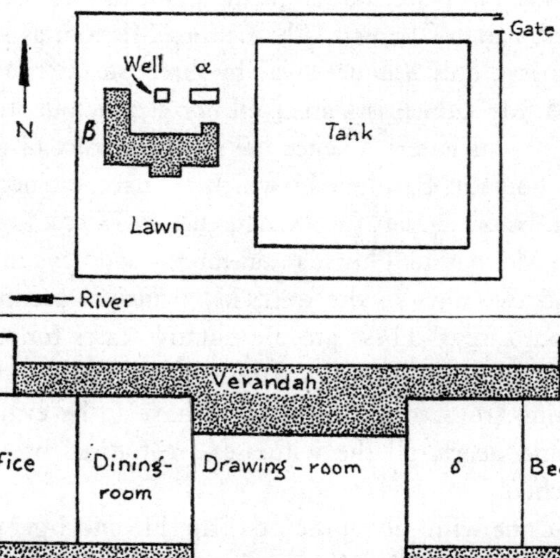

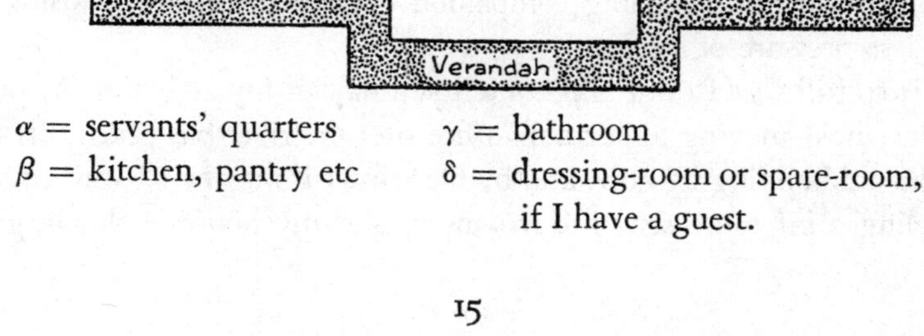

α = servants' quarters
β = kitchen, pantry etc
γ = bathroom
δ = dressing-room or spare-room, if I have a guest.

I haven't indicated the doors, as there are 22 of them and 18 windows!

My furniture arrived safely a few days ago, and looks very nice. The only damage was a crack in one drawer of the dressing-table. I've managed to get some of my curtains, but the durzi is very slow. I'm having an absolute orgy of spending, but I feel it's worth while to make the house as nice as I can.

.... I look forward to hearing whether you saw Mrs. Blank, and got my books and clothes alright. Yesterday I heard, to my great relief, that Wooller of Jalpaiguri has bought Peter. I've let him go for a song, but it's the worst time of year for selling, and I simply had to get him off my hands.

Well, I've finished my air mail pad, and I must now mug up the work that I shall have to do in Faridpur.

Madaripur, East Bengal
18 July 1936

Many thanks for your last letters, the first to be sent here direct. Madaripur is indeed a damp place, but from the point of view of malaria, it's one of the healthiest parts of Bengal. The Oxford Mission, as you observed, has a branch at Barisal, only 8 hours away by direct steamer. I hope to go there some week-end. My launch is neither oil nor electric but steam. (I am going straight through your letters – hence the inconsequence of my sentences.)

I had a few hours at Faridpur in which to make the acquaintance of my Collector, Hill, before he left for a conference in Dacca.....

I spent from Monday to Thursday on tour – two days in the south of the subdivision and two days in the west. My principal occupation was trying 'Bad Livelihood' cases.[23] These are preventative cases for securing the good behaviour of habitual criminals by taking a bond. They are tried in the locality, and anything from 30 to 70 witnesses have to be examined. They are very tedious, and nearly all the witnesses are tutored by the police. I also visited three schools.

Hafizuddin came with me on the first trip. He and I get on well together, and he's a pleasant travelling companion. Touring is quite amusing, and there's less pressure of work.

Life is so full that I can't hope to tell you half of my activities. At present we're very busy moving to our new office site; the river has practically come up to the old building by now, and by the winter it may be all washed away. I'm feeling a bit more settled down now, and my house is slowly getting arranged. A wife would have been really useful these last three weeks! I've little time myself to devote to the house and garden. I'm learning a lot both about my own character and about Bengalis.

Madaripur, East Bengal
27 July 1936

I'm afraid I've missed the usual mail this week, but I thought you'd prefer a long letter a few days late to a scrappy note sent in time. I'm on my way back from a longish tour in the east of my subdivision, and I've got an hour or two to spare before I get back to Madaripur . . . . .

It really is very difficult to give you an idea of my life here, my activities are so multifarious. If I run through my diary for the last 8 days, you'll get some idea.

Sunday 19th. My first peaceful day since coming to M'pur; only did 3 or 4 hours' work, chiefly composing a long report about a recalcitrant old headmaster of the local Girls' High School, who was dismissed for incompetence and misconduct last year, & who is grumbling about his gratuity. Did my first entertaining, having Mr. & Mrs. Boyle to lunch.

Monday 20th. The first day's work in the New Office. My court-room is quite comfortable, and I have a retiring room of my own, the absence of which was a great defect of the old office. These buildings are only temporary. A new permanent site has been selected a couple of miles inland from the river, and I went to see it for the first time that afternoon.[24] It was pleasant to stretch my legs. I get very little time for exercise, and even if I had leisure there is no form of exercise in which I could indulge here. 'Water, water everywhere', and not a road to walk on. In spite of all my touring, my life is really a sedentary one. I shall have to take to Muller in my bathroom.

Tuesday 21st. Usual incessant work from 7-11 in my bungalow and 11.30-5 in my office. At 6.0, presided over a meeting of all the prominent citizens of the town to congratulate the King on his merciful escape.[25] (This meeting was not my suggestion.) Spent the evening with the Boyles at Char Mugria – my first 'night out'. They are very keen Mah Jong players, & I enjoyed reviving my memories of a game which is far too good to have been merely a passing craze.

Wednesday 22nd. A hectic day, which started with a summons to the hospital at 3.30 a.m. to take the dying declaration of a woman who had been half-murdered. I don't know if she's dead yet; she survived till Wednesday evening anyway, so I needn't have been dragged out of bed. Some important letters from Hill & a stream of callers kept me busier than usual that morning, and I was on the go all day, clearing up things before setting out on tour again.

Thursday 23rd. Set off with Hafizuddin in the 'Rosalind' to Naria. Spent the day trying a 'Bad Livelihood' case against 5 habitual thieves; heard 50 witnesses. Also inspected the Boys' High School, which is now one of the best in the subdivision, thanks to a very keen headmaster. Interviewed various local officials, including the Palong Circle Officer, Abdul Rahim,[26] who has been with me all this tour, and whose knowledge of the locality and sound judgement are quite invaluable.

I see that, to make my letters at all intelligible, I shall have to give you a rough map of the subdivision. I don't expect your map of Bengal is on a large enough scale. There are 9 police stations, and 3 Circles.

[The reader is here spared my sketch map and referred to page 8.]

Sibchar Circle	Sibchar P.S.
	Janjira P.S.
Palong Circle	Palong P.S.
	Naria P.S.
	Bhedarganj P.S.
	Gosairhat P.S.
Madaripur Circle	Madaripur P.S.
	Rajair P.S.
	Kalkini P.S.

Palong Circle is the most important of the three, and Janjira is the least important police station.

Friday 24th. Conducted an inquiry into the condition of some latrines which are ranged on either side of a road in Naria. At the moment, they are merely unpleasant, but in the hot weather (when they happened to catch the eye – and nose – of the District Magistrate) they must be nauseating. I directed the proprietors to construct a more hygienic type in a more secluded place. Tried another Bad Livelihood case, which was unduly protracted by a verbose pleader. In the evening held a meeting to collect money for the King's Memorial Fund.

Saturday 25th. Inquired into a petition by some villagers in Bhedarganj, who alleged that all their lands had been washed away by the river in 1930, and that they were being sued for arrears of rent from 1930-33. It was quite impossible to do more than guess, as the river had been steadily encroaching every year, but I decided that they were exaggerating, & that the land in question had gone under in '34. Then I went on to a pleasant village called Panditsar, with a really encouraging High School, and the nicest 'atmosphere' I've struck yet – a refreshing absence of the usual party factions. While I was there, I opened their new 'Village Hall', which is not larger than the gentlemen's cloakroom in the Waldershare Village Hall.

Sunday 27th. Spent the morning in an enquiry into the proceedings of a Union Board[27] election. The allegations against the Circle Officer who had conducted the election proceedings were a tissue of lies. In the afternoon, I held my first big public function – a meeting of the Constitutional League, whose main purpose is to rouse public opinion against terrorism. There was quite a good gathering, but half-way through, a heavy down-pour of rain & violent wind made the speakers quite inaudible. I had managed to get my first Bengali speech off my chest – a nerve-racking ordeal. I dined yesterday evening with the zemindar of Kartikpur,[28] the wealthiest landowner in the subdivision, and a member of the old Mahommedan aristocracy.

There must be much in this letter which puzzles you, so do ask lots of questions in your letters. The affairs of this place are so much a part of my life that I sometimes take for granted knowledge which you have not got.

By the way, I did tell you that I sold Peter, didn't I? Certainly he'd have been no more use than a rocking-horse here.

Just returned, to find your letters of the 17th. Glad to hear that Father has got into the garden. To answer Mother's questions (1) I haven't taken to a pipe yet, and have no yearning for it either. I still smoke my occasional Turkish cigarette after dinner. (2) I've put my camera away for the rains, as it's impossible to get good results at this time of year. So I'm afraid you'll have to wait till the autumn to get a *visual* impression of Madaripur.

Madaripur, East Bengal
2 August 1936

I've again missed the usual mail, but I think in future I must write my letters on Sundays as I can guarantee no spare time on Saturdays. You may, if you find it convenient, write by the Tuesday mail instead of the Friday one. . . .

. . . .This has not been an easy week. I know you like to hear about the clouds as well as the silver lining, so I'll always try to give you a true impression of my life here. First of all, the weather's been beastly all this week, heavy rain every day. I slosh along to Office in Wellington boots. Secondly, my nice young pani-wallah has had to return to Rajshahi over some criminal litigation, and I've had to dismiss him as the case will go on for months; then my bearer's been laid up with a bad knee all the week, and my cook went down with fever yesterday. I've managed to get hold of a man with dirty clothes and a squint, who does his best, but I don't want to keep him longer than I can help. As I've had one of the Oxford Mission Fathers staying for the week-end, it's not been too easy from the domestic point of view.

Thirdly, the work this week has been impossibly heavy. I got back from tour on Monday, and from then till now, I've just worked and eaten and slept and nothing else. However, it won't always be as heavy as this. The chief reason for the extra pressure has been the big Palong case which I probably mentioned in one of my earliest letters from here. Wednesday, Thursday and Friday were spent in cross-examination. It's a most interesting case & is being hotly contested every inch of the way.

The allegation is that a certain Abdul Gafur Kotwal abducted a girl; on the pretext of taking her to see the Chairman of the District Board[29] as a candidate for a course of midwifery, he took her in a boat and molested her. She was rescued by a passing boat. The defence case is that all the prosecution witnesses are Congress people of Palong, who are out to get rid of Abdul Gafur, who is the leader of the Government party in Palong, & have brought this false case for that purpose. As executive officer, I know something of the factions in Palong, which are very bitter.

Palong is the most important section of my subdivision, and this case will have a big effect on my administration here. It shows clearly how difficult it is to be an executive and judicial officer combined. Also, the fact that the case is turning into a political one, Congress v Government, makes it doubly important for me to give a really careful impartial judgement. I'm not having the final say, but merely deciding whether the case is to be committed to the Sessions Court or not.

On Wednesday, I cross-examined the girl from 2-5. On Thursday, 5 more witnesses from 12 till 6.30, including the mother, who fainted dramatically; and finished the remaining 8 witnesses on Friday from 2 till 7.30. You can imagine that this on top of my ordinary work has been a big strain. The case is now adjourned to a couple of days at the end of the month for defence witnesses.

Other preoccupations have been the Girls' High School, which, like all the other institutions of this place, is riddled with faction. On the 7th & 8th, the District Magistrate & Inspectress of Schools are coming to try to set the matter finally at rest. Preparations for the Dist. Magte's visit have been another little addition of work.

The people here are so *helpless*, and so factious. They haven't begun to grasp the principle of attaining an object by co-operation, and they seek membership of public bodies simply in order to increase their own prestige, and not from any sense of doing useful work. The Municipality, the School Committees, the Union Boards – all are the same; their energies are wasted in trying to down each other. Wirepulling and backbiting are their chief hobbies. Those who are supporters of Government are mostly impractical idealists. As the S.D.O. is one of the few people known to be impartial, an enormous amount of work is done by him which could, and in any normal country would, be done by private persons. The high officials of Govt. increase our work without increasing our staff; every Magte. & every clerk is overworked, yet there are hundreds of people crying out for clerkships; and at the same time, the chief criticism of Govt. is the gross expense of administration, which will be increased still further by additional staff.

Well, that's enough grousing, and I've got many things to be thankful for; good health, a good house, and ample pay.

Father Fawssett of the Oxford Mission came to stay on Friday evening & is leaving tonight. I haven't had a minute to entertain him properly, and it would really have been much more convenient if he'd stayed at Charmugria. He's really rather a dry old stick, the result of living alone among outcaste Hindus for the last 7 years.[30] However, I've enjoyed seeing him. And the Communion Service at Charmugria was most refreshing. There were only two other communicants, one Armenian and one Mr. Lawrence, a jute merchant who's been at Charmugria on and off since *1898*, and is a real Christian.

The international situation is even worse than usual. I don't know what to make of the fighting in Spain.

Much love to you both. I'll try not to be so depressing next week.

Madaripur, East Bengal
9 August 1936

This has been an interesting week, busy as usual but busy in a different way. Hafizuddin and I left on the 4th for Kartikpur in the east of the subdivision, to meet the District Magistrate & the Superintendent of Police, Doha.[31] The Military Intelligence Officer, Major Ansell, also appeared on the scene, so it was quite a foregathering of officials. Our host was Gyasuddin Ahmed, the wealthy zemindar to whom I referred last week. On the 4th we watched a sports display on a very muddy ground; fortunately it was not actually raining at the time. On the 5th there was a big public meeting followed by the local school prize-giving. We all left for Madaripur the next day. Hill has been here for the last three days, and only left last night. He & Doha stayed on their launch and Ansell put up in my bungalow. Hill spent the time inspecting various institutions of Madaripur – not of my office, which he's put off till next week, when he's paying us another visit. I followed him round for most of the time, & only went to office in the afternoons – a welcome change. Yesterday we spent 5 solid hours trying to settle the affairs of the Girls' School – I think & hope we've got rid of the old ex-headmaster at last; he was a regular plague, and, being as deaf as a post, very difficult to deal with.

There were dinner parties all three nights. Hafizuddin was the host on the 6th, I on the 7th, & the Boyles yesterday. My dinner-party went off quite well, though 9 guests was too many for my small house & my china & cutlery. I have six of everything, and beyond that I have to borrow.

I've now had a good opportunity to get to know Hill. He's grey-haired, though not over 40; sharp blue eyes; very crooked back; a nice smile; an exact, terse manner of speaking. He's hardworking and efficient; he makes me feel I'm very inefficient, but I think he realizes my inexperience is an excuse. We haven't got many tastes in common, but I like him. Doha is a very different pair of shoes; Dey had a strong dislike of him & told me all his suspicions as soon as I arrived; Doha realizes this, and thinks I am prejudiced against him, but I'm trying not to be.

The river has risen at least a foot this week, and my house is practically surrounded by water. My Wellingtons have been invaluable. Tomorrow I shall start going to office by boat. The effect of my insulation is to make my house a refuge for ants.

.....This letter is badly put together. I meant to write earlier in the day, but my arrears of work have kept me busy, and now it is late and I am rather sleepy.

Madaripur, East Bengal
15 August 1936

I've no time to write this letter, but don't see any prospect of any leisure during the next few days, so, as your letters have just arrived, I may as well scrawl off a few lines in answer, as I can thus catch the early Air Mail.

Tomorrow is the date of the Union Board Conference, and all the big officials of the District are gathered together for it. I'm putting up Doha (the

Superintendent of Police) and also the S.D.O. Goalundo, called Ali.[32] The business of organizing has been a considerable addition to my already heavy work. On top of this the Collector's inspecting my office on Monday & Tuesday, and the Commissioner (a *very* big bug) on the 28th. If I can get through this month I can get through anything!

There are a fine lot of questions for me to answer, but I can only tackle a few. First, 'Madaripur, East Bengal' is sufficient address. (2) I have tea & toast & fruit at 6.0, & 'breakfast-cum-lunch' at 10.30 or 11.0.[33] This is the same arrangement as at Rajshahi, & is the only one compatible with office hours of 11 to 5.

(3) The river is the Arial Khan, a tributary of the Ganges. The water is fresh but filthy; it is tidal even here. There are excellent edible fish,[34] & fishing is a possible sport – if one had any leisure. My tank is full of leeches, so the Doctor doesn't advise swimming. I might get it cleaned. (4) I put my camera away because the damp affects the films.

. . . It's been like a greenhouse the last few days, & I'm sweating like a pig as I write. But the river's subsided & my house is no longer an island.

Madaripur, East Bengal
22 August 1936

I only had time to scrawl off a line to you last week. The week-end Conferences went off without any major mishap, which is a comfort. I must admit I've seldom felt so completely depressed and tired out as I did that week-end. But I'm getting more confidence in myself now. I had the matter out with Hill, and explained that if Govt. had chosen to send me to one of the heaviest and most difficult subdivisions of Bengal as my first charge, they must expect a certain amount of inefficiency my first few months. But I'm learning fast. I'm also beginning to realize just what the Government is up against, with these Bengali people. I'm not a person who sees a man's faults rather than his virtues, but it really can't be denied that the 'upper classes' of this subdivision are a pretty nasty lot on the whole. . . .[35] The more I see of the schools, the more I realize that the educational system is wrong from top to bottom – mere cramming shops, with all the boys' intellectual energy sapped by having to work in a foreign language – all the work in the upper classes of the High Schools is done in English.

I've just come back from a tour of two days in the north of the subdivision – Sibchar. It's the quietest area. I presided over one school prize-giving, and opened one village dispensary among other things. The sun shone most of the time – a welcome change – and I wished I had had my camera with me. I must get it out again, now that the Rains are nearly over.

The next joy is the Commissioner's visit. He will be here from the 27th to the 29th. He is one of the very senior members of the Service, came out here about 1906, Nelson by name, a great authority on Settlement work.[36]

The river reached a great height on Wednesday. The whole of my compound is ankle-deep in water. I have to go everywhere by boat. There will probably be one more big rise, and then the worst will be over. The water will subside, and my garden will be a mass of stinking mud. The houses of most of the inhabitants of the town are under water; it's the worst flood since 1931. But the East Bengali is amphibious, and a mild flood doesn't really upset him much. By the way, the embankment at Rajshahi has broken, so I expect my friends there are in a worse plight still.

This letter is not well strung together. There is so much to say, and you have so little knowledge of what this country is like, that I find it very hard to describe the kind of life I'm living. Ask me lots of questions.

Madaripur, East Bengal
5 September 1936

Many thanks for your letters of the *21*st August, which arrived this evening – a week late. . . .

Life goes on much the same here, Busy isn't the word for it. Thank Heavens this big abduction case will soon be over. I've just come back from hearing the arguments in it (7 hours!), conducted by two of the leading Calcutta advocates.[37] I shall do little for the next three days except write my decision. The vernacular Press are making a lot of the case. It would take far too long to begin to explain all the subtle intricacies of the case, which involves the corruptness & prejudices of half the Govt. officials in the district. There's been so much perjury on both sides, and so many false documents produced that I hardly know which way to turn.

Yesterday I was out on tour – a busy programme. In the morning, an enquiry into allegations against a zemindar who had, I found, failed to pay many of his rural police officers[38] under his charge, and got false receipts from them. In the afternoon, I went to a school run by and for the depressed classes, miles from anywhere.[39] It was a 3 hours' journey each way in a small 'country boat'. I shall soon (October perhaps) be taking my camera out again, & I hope to send you a few pictures of some of the things I see in the course of my tours. It takes such a long time to describe in a letter a single incident, let alone to give you the background of rural Bengal.

Today came a complete surprise, which sounds almost Providential, in the shape of a letter from Sir Wm. Barton, asking whether I'd like to take on the job of private tutor to the heir to the throne of Mysore! It's a life-changing decision, and I haven't been able to consider it yet, but it looks rather like a solution to the problems I put in my last week's letter. I shall be writing to Sir Wm. as soon as I get breathing-space. It's extraordinarily kind of him to have thought of suggesting me, & I fancy I'd be a fool to turn down the chance.

This must go to the post. How lovely for you to know the *date* of Margaret's homecoming.

as from Madaripur, East Bengal
13 September 1936

Just time for a short letter before I turn in tonight. I'm in the middle of the longest tour I've done yet – altogether 6 days away from headquarters. The 'Rosalind' is anchored in a *khal* (small river) in Bhedarganj at the moment, and except for the fluttering of the numerous jute-moths and the occasional creak of oars it is very peaceful and pleasantly cool. My work on this tour has been to inspect Union Boards and Schools, & to hold one or two public meetings in connection with educational improvement and rural reconstruction. Oh that I could talk Bengali fluently! One feels so helpless in the interior of the subdivision. I can of course understand & make myself understood, but all the time I feel an alien.[40]

The first half of the week was occupied with little but the judgement in the Palong case. I spent the whole of Sunday at Madaripur, & the whole of Monday in the launch on the way to Faridpur drafting my judgement, and the whole of Tuesday morning typing it out – 14 pages, foolscap size. Tuesday afternoon was fixed for the District Board meeting, which was a dull affair, but provided the excuse for a trip to Faridpur. The only comic side was that the principal defence witness and the principal accused in the case were the Chairman and a member of the District Board respectively, so I had to keep a very 'poker' face. At Faridpur, the S.P. (Doha) and Hill each gave dinner-parties, but otherwise it was a pretty tedious visit. I travelled back on Wednesday, and delivered the judgement on Thursday. The court-room was packed and the excitement when I gave the order discharging all three accused was considerable. The prosecution are of course appealing to the Sessions Judge to set aside my order, but I expected them to do that. The Sessions Judge is believed to be very biased in favour of the prosecution, and if he does set aside my order I shall know this to be true, for on the evidence there's not a shadow of doubt that the case was a false one.[41]

. . . It's late and I must go to bed. I've not *yet* found time to write to Sir Wm. Barton & the Mysore Minister & Resident, but I've definitely decided to write. . . .

Madaripur, East Bengal
20 September 1936

The Saumarez Smith family is in the wars, and no mistake! Father condemned to 3 more months' idleness,[42] Mother sorely tried by a domestic upheaval – and then I added to your troubles by writing my excessively gloomy letter of the 31st August. Things are better now, but I'm out of sympathy with the whole system. We're trying to impose a Western constitution on an Eastern mentality, and it just doesn't fit. So, though I continue to work day in and day out, I haven't really got my heart in the work.

Did I tell you last week that my 2nd officer, Bardhan,[43] had been transferred at a moment's notice to Chittagong? The 3rd officer, a Muslim called Latif, has been promoted to 2nd officer. He's not such an attractive personality as Bardhan, but he's got a great knowledge of the law. Bardhan's gap has not yet been filled, so we are short-handed & the criminal files are getting badly in arrears. The only blessing is that I shall be able to get away for the Pujas.[44] I think I shall go up to Shillong if the Blanks will have me, but I haven't written yet.

My gramophone records have come from Imhof's at last. They were held up for 2 months for some unknown reason, but better late than never. I play a record or two at meal-times, as that is my only spare time. I ordered the first three albums of the Columbia History of Music, 8 records in each album. The first album, which is the only one I've allowed myself to hear yet, has some lovely madrigals & early virginals music, & a fine Sanctus by Palestrina.

I've definitely taken steps about the Mysore project. I wrote on Wednesday to Sir Wm. Barton, the Chief Minister of Mysore, & the present Resident of Mysore. Naturally I haven't had time for a reply yet, but I think I may be able to escape from this place before Christmas.

I returned on Wednesday from 6 days' touring – my longest trip so far. Of course there was an appalling accumulation of files on my return. During the 6 days, I held 3 public meetings, inspected 3 schools, 4 Union Board offices, and 1 Dispensary, and examined more than 30 witnesses in a 'bad livelihood' case. So even my trips to the mofussil are not rest-cures!

'The Bridge' that you referred to is the Howrah Bridge, which connects the main city of Calcutta with its industrial satellite Howrah. Oddly enough, in spite of my many visits to Calcutta, I've never yet seen the bridge. There's been tremendous discussion whether the contract should be given to an Indian firm or not. Eventually, the Indian firm lost the contract.

Well, my dears, it's nearly midnight & I must go to bed. Keep your spirits up & I'll keep up mine.

Madaripur, East Bengal
27 September 1936

I'm in the launch on the way to Sibchar, to hold a couple of public meetings. I've been at headquarters all this week, and there's practically nothing to write about. Apart from a couple of important school committee meetings and the endless routine of writing and receiving letters and memorandums and orders and files, my chief work was writing a very difficult judgement on a 'bad livelihood' case. If a man can be proved to be a *habitual* thief, he can be bound down for a period up to 3 years to be of good behaviour. The original intention of the law was preventive and not punitive, but the present practice is quite otherwise. A man who is convicted in a 'B.L.' case almost invariably goes to jail, as any sureties he seeks to produce are declared unfit.

This particular case was against no less than 6 accused, all suspected of being habitual thieves. The case started in February, since which time accused have been waiting in jail, and appearing periodically as the case slowly moved on. There were 75 prosecution witnesses and 40 defence witnesses, and only about half-a-dozen reliable people in the whole bunch. The trouble was that one innocent man had been involved, out of party faction. He was defended by the ablest lawyer of the Madaripur bar[45] – these cases are usually undefended – and another effect was that lots of respectable people of the locality refused to come forward and give evidence against the other 5 who I'm pretty sure were thieves. The result was that I had to let off 3 of them. It was a rotten case from beginning to end, and I wrote a rotten judgement.

... Forgive a short and dull letter. I find it difficult to write interestingly to you, as I am living in a world of chaprassis and chaukidars and '144' cases and tadbir and A.G.B.'s objections and D.W.s[46] and other things of which you know nothing & can care little.

P.S. Just returned from tour to find your letters awaiting me. . . . If I get the Mysore job (about which I've heard nothing more yet) it certainly doesn't mean my sundering my connection with the I.C.S.

Madaripur, East Bengal
4 October 1936

I'm just off on a week's tour, in Palong Circle, with the District Magistrate, followed by a trip to Faridpur for the monthly District Board meeting. The chief event this week has been a visit from the District Judge. I came back from tour on the 29th, and he arrived on the 30th & stayed for four days. He was chiefly concerned with the Civil Courts,[47] but he had a look at the criminal side too. We were both very friendly to each other outwardly, but 'inwardly we were as ravening wolves' owing to the Palong abduction case, to which I've often referred before. It's a queer triangle of forces in this district – the Superintendent of Police fighting the District Judge, with Madaripur as the battle-ground. And I trying not to take sides with either party, but to keep some faint regard for truth & justice.

I went over to Charmugria yesterday afternoon, to see the High School & preside over a Committee Meeting. I took the chance of an evening with the Boyles, which was a pleasant relief.

No word from Mysore yet. I'm definitely going to Shillong for the Pujas – bless the Blanks!

Today I had an unusual experience. Hafizuddin's daughter had just attained the age for going on solid food, and I was invited to the ceremony of 'Khir Khilai'. This consisted of a short religious ceremony followed by a large dinner. Everything was done in Indian style (H. usually lives in European style), and I was amused to see all the Moslem officials cast off their officialdom. It's the first time (*mirabile dictu*) that I've had a proper Indian meal since I've been in India. That is to say, squatting on the floor, and eating with one's fingers. My knees were a bit stiff at the end, but it was well worth it. . . .

P.S. We had a small cyclone today, but it didn't do any damage.

as from Madaripur, East Bengal
10 October 1936

I'm actually writing from Hill's bungalow at Faridpur, as I am here for one of my monthly District Board meetings. I've been out on tour all this week, with the District Magistrate. On Monday he came with Doha, and

Major Ansell the Military Intelligence Officer, to preside over a prize-giving at one of the few financially sound and well-run schools of Palong Circle. The next day we parted company, and the 3 'burra sahibs' went to inspect one of the worst schools, while Hafizuddin and I went to continue a 'B.L.' case which I had started in September. On our return that night, Hafizuddin was stricken with violent internal pains. He must have eaten something which disagreed with him, but we'd had identical food that day, except that he'd taken one sweet cake at a tea-party given by the local zemindar. The next morning he was much better, but the doctor told him he'd better return to Madaripur. (It was very lucky that we'd halted for the night in a place which boasted of a qualified doctor). So on Wednesday, Hafizuddin went back with the 'Rosalind', and I transferred to the Collector's[48] launch, 'Mollie', a much larger and more comfortable launch.

The real object of the Collector's visit was to inspect the *char* areas. A char is an island formed by alluvion as a river changes its course. Every year fresh land is formed and old land is washed away. When a new char rises out of the river there is a rush to settle on it. The char people are lawless and primitive. They build houses on stilts. The Government is the principal landlord. One of the main Govt. tenants had been getting very much above himself, and had been occupying large areas of land belonging to other poorer men, without paying a pice of rent, and generally speaking he considered himself to be the uncrowned king of the locality. Hill came to show him that he wasn't, and we got him to sign a document promising to pay up all the arrear rents, to surrender all the lands of which he had not taken settlement, and to abide by the Collector's decision in all the matters under dispute. We visited his house on Thursday morning (it was the only substantial building within miles), and he presented this document to Hill, in the presence of all his relatives and a large gathering of venerable bearded Mussalmans. It was an interesting visit, and one felt something of the older spirit of the Company days, when the Collector really was an autocrat.[49]

Next week I shall be very busy for the first few days catching up the accumulations of work of the past week, and trying to get things straight before the Pujas. I have one more tour in the north of the subdivision and then – off to Shillong! Still not a word from Mysore, but the cold weather is coming, and even Madaripur will be tolerable in the cold weather.

Unfortunately I've not got your latest letters with me, but I'm glad to think Father is safe at home again, & able to do a little parochial work. It won't be long now before Margaret's return, and that hope will keep you both going during the winter. . .

P.S. Just found your letters. In case it isn't clear to you, let me give more details about the Mysore proposal. I wrote to the Minister & the Resident on 16th September asking for further particulars about the job – e.g. pay. I shall of course remain in the I.C.S. & be lent to the Govt. of Mysore. I knew that Sir Wm. B. was Resident of Mysore for 5 years; it was on the strength of that that he was able to recommend my name to the Minister & Maharaja at all. I also knew that Mysore is one of the best & most progressive of all the Native States & that the Maharaja is an exceptionally enlightened man. I can't say anything about leave, but you know that I shall do my very utmost to get leave in 1938. I'm toying with the idea of taking a month's leave (if I get the job) & going to Mysore via Singapore. But this is a sheer castle in the air.

Madaripur, East Bengal
17 October 1936

Excuse the odd notepaper. I came out on tour without making any preparations for correspondence, and I am taking advantage of a leisure hour before returning to the whirl of Madaripur. I haven't got your letters with me to answer either. . . . Father's letter asked a string of questions about Mysore, apparently assuming that I'd got the job, which is very far from the case yet. I was disappointed to receive a cold, formal letter from Col. Plowden's Secretary referring me for information to the Maharaja's Private Secretary. As Sir Wm. Barton had told me Col. P. was a personal friend of his, this was a bit of a blow. However, I was much cheered two days ago to receive a wire from Sir Mirza Ismail[50] acknowledging his recent receipt of my letter on his return from Europe, and saying that he would write soon.

I still don't know on what day I shall be leaving for Shillong, owing to an annoying visit impending from Sir Nazimuddin,[51] a Member of the Executive Council. He is coming to my subdivision tomorrow and to Madaripur itself on the 19th, on a purely electioneering campaign. (He is going all out to be the first Prime Minister under the New Constitution).[52] If he were coming on an official visit, I should have to make colossal preparations, as a Member of the Exec. Council is second only to the Governor. But a civilian is supposed to have no political views, so I shall certainly not attend any of Sir Nazimuddin's meetings. But I don't feel I can leave M'pur altogether until he's quit of the place.

I got back from Faridpur last Sunday evening after a long & tedious journey. Monday was a wild rush, as is often the case when I return from a long tour. The chief event was a Committee Meeting of the main Mahommedan High School, which is hopelessly in debt & very badly administered by a corrupt old Zemindar who should never have been elected Secretary. On Tuesday, I presided over the prize-giving ceremony of the Madaripur School, one of the largest in the District. Wednesday was a public holiday, which was a great relief, as I managed to get through a lot of arrear correspondence. Then I escaped on tour again, which was rather wicked of me, as the last days before the Puja holidays will be very busy as far as Court work is concerned. But I'd planned my tour long before, and I'm visiting a part of the subdivision I've not seen at all before, up in the north-east.[53] It's an entirely Muslim population, & much of it is 'char' land, so the people are very backward. When I return from this tour I shall have been to nearly all parts of the subdivision – sketchily of course. I've just been giving a cinema display on an outfit lent (complete with operator) by the District Magistrate. I showed short films on Jaipur, the Taj Mahal, & the Jubilee Procession. It was quite a successful show. My next letter will be from Shillong.

Notes

[1] Mrs. Blank was the wife of Mr. A. L. Blank, I.C.S., who had been District Judge of Rajshahi during my first four months there. He was then transferred to Shillong, as Judicial Secretary and Legal Remembrancer to the Government of Assam. I had spent a week's holiday with them in Shillong in May 1935. They had three schoolgirl daughters in England. Later Mr. Blank became a Judge of the Calcutta High Court.

[2] Susil Kumar Dey joined the I.C.S. in Bengal in 1930. He had been at Madaripur for sixteen months.

[3] Touring in the *Rosalind*, a small steam launch, was one of the pleasantest sides of the work. The 'sahibs' ' accommodation consisted of a small saloon cabin, a two-berth bedroom cabin, and a minute 'bathroom'. There was a crew of four – the serang, a venerable figure rather like the Bellman in 'The Hunting of the Snark'; the engineer; the mate; and the serang's son, whose principal duty was (literally) swinging the lead. When the Subdivisional Police Officer and I were touring together, with a bearer apiece, plus one or two orderlies, there must have been nearly a dozen souls on board.

[4] Deputy Magistrates were members of the Bengal Civil Service. This, with a cadre of about 230, was in an intermediate position between the members of the Indian Civil Service in Bengal (with a cadre of 185), and the Bengal Junior Civil Service, with a cadre of about 540. When I went to Madaripur, there were two Deputy Magistrates there – the Second Officer, Babu Niranjan Bardhan (a Hindu), and the Third Officer, Maulvi Abdul Latif (a Muslim).

[5] K. A. L. Hill had joined the I.C.S. in Bengal in 1922, He had become District Magistrate of Faridpur in February 1936, having spent a good deal of his earlier service in Land Settlement work.

The chief executive official of a District was referred to as the District Magistrate in his magisterial and other work, and as the Collector in his land revenue work. He was also generically referred to as the District Officer, or, with the prevalent passion for initials, as the D.M. . In some less developed parts of the Province, e.g. the Chittagong Hill Tracts, he was called the Deputy Commissioner.

[6] Books in Bengal needed constant care. If neglected during the monsoon, the covers (this was before paperbacks) acquired a sort of grey fungus; and throughout the year they were liable to the ravages of burrowing fish-insects. Glass-fronted bookcases were essential. All this, combined with frequent changes of appointment – it was unusual to stay for more than three years in the same station – militated against building up a library.

[7] Arthur Wooller joined the I.C.S. in Bengal in 1935 and moved to the Indian Political Service in 1939. When India became independent in 1947, he, like many other members of the Indian Civil and Political Services, was taken into the Diplomatic Service. He married the eldest daughter of the Blanks.

[8] A bearer was one's senior domestic servant, a combined valet and butler. At Madaripur, I had a staff of four – the absolute minimum! – bearer, cook, 'masalchi' (scullion), and sweeper. My bearer, Hedayet Ali, a Muslim from North Bihar, had been bearer to Mr. Burge, the third of the Midnapore District Magistrates to be assassinated by terrorists. He joined me when I first went to Rajshahi, staying with me until 1942.

[9] With a plethora of railway porters, one did not travel light when moving to a new station and an unfurnished bungalow. But I find it hard to imagine how I needed *thirty* pieces of luggage! However, here is an attempt at a list:

1. An enormous tin-lined trunk, which required four coolies to carry it.
2. A standard tin-lined cabin trunk.
3. A leather Revelation suitcase (a twenty-first birthday present, still going strong).
4. A camp-bed.
5. A bedding-roll (indispensable for all overnight journeys in Indian trains).
6. A camp folding table.
7. A camp folding chair.
8. A camp folding washstand.
9. A commode. (When I first went to Rajshahi, I had not acquired this essential article of furniture, with embarrassing consequences.)
10. A zinc (?) hip-bath.
11. A green canvas bag, for dirty clothes.
12. A tea-chest, for china and kitchen utensils.

13, 14. Two tea-chests, for books.

15. A Remington portable typewriter (see Letter of 24 May 1937).
16. A Petromax lamp.
17. A bicycle.
18. A topi box.

That only accounts for a little more than half – and the three servants' luggage certainly would not have made up the remainder.

[10] In more detail, the furniture consisted of: a sofa and two armchairs, a dining-table and six chairs, a glass-fronted bookcase, and a dressing-table with an attached mirror. At less that £27, this was indeed 'a really magnificent bargain'. (Rs. 40/- was worth £3.)

[11] The Revd. F. W. Douglass (1866-1949) was one of the best-known of the Oxford Mission Fathers, particularly for his work at Behala, on the southern outskirts of Calcutta. He worked there from 1909 until his death, living ascetically in a mud-floored wall-less thatched hut. I am only one of many hundreds of 'all sorts and conditions' of men and women who saw in 'Father D' the vision of a truly Christ-like life.

[12] Eric Kitchin was an exact contemporary of mine, and we had shared a bungalow in Rajshahi the previous year as fellow Assistant Magistrates.

[13] The other five 'Europeans' – the term seems odd now, but was the standard term used to describe people who were not Indians or Anglo-Indians – all lived in Charmugria: the Boyles and three jute-merchants.

[14] A. K. M. Hafizuddin, to whom this book is dedicated, joined the Indian Police in 1933. He appears constantly in the letters, and reappears in the Envoi.

[15] Babu Gurudas Banerji, who was my confidential clerk until laid low with pleurisy the following June, was of tremendous assistance. He was quite young, had an excellent command of English, and was wholly trustworthy. The 'Bengali Babu' was mocked by Kipling: without him, the Government of Bengal would have instantly collapsed.

Much of Gurudas Babu's work was not confidential; he was really a Personal Assistant. But his files were kept in my bungalow, and not in the Subdivisional Office. One regular chore was the 'fortnightly confidential report' to the District Magistrate, which was a general 'situation report' about anything interesting happening in the subdivision. The morning period was the main time for people to come and see me – once I was in the office, I was too busy with Court work. They would not make an appointment, but wait at the other end of the bungalow verandah and send their names in through my orderly. Their business was infinitely varied: one might be a member of some School Committee, another a visitor from an outlying part of the subdivision wanting a tube-well, a third an official of the Public Works Department paying his respects while passing through Madaripur.

[16] The Jail was very handy for the old office-buildings near the bank of the eroding river, but with the move to the new buildings later that month, it became rather off the beaten track, and I used not to visit it more than once or twice a week. It was effectively in charge of the Jail Clerk.

[17] Madaripur was as active educationally as it was politically – the two went hand-in-hand – and there must have been at least a dozen high schools. They could become centres of disaffection – hence the S.D.O.'s involvement in them.

[18] This steamer would have been a small paddle-steamer, belonging to the River Steam Navigation Company (of which Mr. Boyle was the local Agent), plying up the Palong River to the steamer-station, Tarpasa. There I changed to a larger and very comfortable vessel sailing on the mainstream of the Ganges/Padma/Meghna River. This took me to Goalundo, from which there was a short railway journey to Faridpur. In the monsoon, the main river was at least two miles from bank to bank.

[19] The nearest equivalent to the District Board in English local government was the County Council, but the parallel is not close, as the District Board's powers and finances were limited. Nevertheless, they were the training grounds for the Provincial Legislative Assembly. All the members were elected, except for the four Subdivisional Officers. The District Magistrate was *not* a member.

[20] The Marwaris, a Hindu community from Rajputana, occupied a most prominent position in trade, commerce and moneylending throughout Bengal, and in many other parts of the Indian sub-continent.

[21] I have virtually no recollection of the activities of the Co-operative Bank, except for interminable arguments about the position of Co-operative Societies washed away by diluvion. Its chief executive was an official with a face heavily pitted with smallpox, who used to put 'I.C.S.' after his name, which in *his* case stood for 'Inspector of Co-operative Societies'.

[22] Whenever a house was built in this part of Bengal, the first step was to excavate a large reservoir or 'tank'. The earth from this raised the ground level around the house above (normal) flood-level.

[23] 'Bad livelihood' cases were governed by section 110 of the Criminal Procedure Code, which ran:

> Whenever a Presidency Magistrate, District Magistrate, or Subdivisional Magistrate receives information that any person within the local limits of his jurisdiction

(a) is by habit a robber, housebreaker, thief or forger or....

(f) is so desperate and dangerous as to render his being at large without security hazardous to the community,

such Magistrate may, in manner hereinafter provided, require such person to show cause why he should not be ordered to execute a bond, with sureties, for his good behaviour for such period, not exceeding three years, as the Magistrate thinks fit to fix.

[24] The site was at a village called Sakuni. Preparations for the move of the subdivisional headquarters there occupied a good deal of my time. See also Envoi.

[25] On July 16th a fanatic had thrown a loaded revolver at King Edward VIII on Constitution Hill, when he was returning to Buckingham Palace after presenting new Colours to the Brigade of Guards.

[26] Circle Officers were members of the Bengal Junior Civil Service, and played a vital part in the executive administration. They did no court work, though criminal complaints were often sent to them for preliminary investigation. When I was on tour, the Circle Officer concerned nearly always accompanied me. They sent me fortnightly confidential reports of their work, which both helped me to know what was going on, and provided much material for my own fortnightly confidential report to the District Magistrate. Maulvi Abdul Rahim was a particularly pleasant and efficient young officer.

[27] A Union Board was the lowest unit of local self-government. It covered an area of ten or a dozen villages, so there were about ninety Union Boards in the subdivision. The Chairman and members were all elected. Their compulsory powers were the appointment, pay and control of the rural police – to be distinguished from the regular police at the nine thanas, or police-stations. A typical Union Board would have half-a-dozen 'chaukidars', under one head 'daffadar'. In addition, an enterprising Union Board, if it was prepared to levy additional rates, could do much for the well-being of the area – improving village roads, sinking tube-wells, even running a modest dispensary. The inspection of Union Boards was a regular feature of my touring work.

[28] Maulvi Gyasuddin Ahmed, who in April 1937 became the Member of the Legislative Assembly for the constituency of East Madaripur.

[29] I cannot remember the proper name of the Chairman, as he was invariably known by his nickname 'Badshah Mia' (Badshah means Emperor). He was a landowner in the north of the subdivision, an ambitious young man – almost as young as me – as evidenced by his election to the Chairmanship of the District Board; he was not very well-educated.

[30] Father Fawssett worked at Jobarpar, a village out-station of the main Oxford Mission work at Barisal.

[31] Mr. A. H. M. Shams-ud-Doha had joined the Indian Police in Bengal in 1924. He enjoyed the unusual distinction for a Muslim of proficiency in Sanskrit. In any district, the three most important officials were the District Magistrate and the District Judge, both normally members of the I.C.S.: and the Superintendent of Police, normally a member of the Indian Police.

[32] Mr. M. H. Ali, I.C.S., 1931–47. He was S.D.O. Goalundo from June 1934 to February 1937.

[33] Among the flotsam of my papers from India that have survived, I discovered inexplicably my order-book to Mazda's, 'the premier wine and provision store' of Calcutta. I used to order my groceries once a month, to supplement what was not available in the local bazaar. Here is a typical order for September 1936:

1 1-lb tin of Huntley & Palmer's Ginger Nuts
3 packets Post Toasties
1 packet Shredded Wheat
2 bottles Kia-Ora lemon squash

2 bottles Rose's Lime Juice
¼ lb cooking cheese
3 1-lb tins of Polson's Butter
2 1-lb tins of margarine
1 1-lb tin of Cadbury's Chocolate
2 medium tins of Pascal's Crème de Menthe
½ lb C & B Almonds without shells
1 1-lb tin of Lipton's Pure Empire Coffee
1 1-lb packet of Rungneet's Flowery Orange Pekoe Tea
2 tins of Cooper's Oxford Marmalade
1 2-lb tin of Morton's lump sugar
3 tins of Nestle's Thick Cream (small)
2 tins Del Monte's large white asparagus
1 bottle Mazda's white pepper
1 bottle Worcester sauce (small) L & P
1 bottle anchovy sauce (small) C & B
1 bottle tomato ketchup (small) Heinz
1 tin McVitie & Price Round Scottish Shortbread.

[34] A particularly good fish was the hilsa, with the flavour of a trout.

[35] This is a naïve generalization, which I was greatly tempted to omit altogether. I had lived a fairly sheltered life in England, and at Rajshahi I was still under training. Now for the first time in a position of responsibility and power, I was learning how people behave, not simply in East Bengal, but all the world over. Indeed, I remember being much cheered (paradoxically) by reading at that time Susil Dey's copy of Winifred Holtby's novel *South Riding*, in which wire-pulling was portrayed on a much larger scale than in Madaripur!

[36] The Province of Bengal was divided into five Divisions, each in charge of a Commissioner. Faridpur was one of the four districts of Dacca Division. The Commissioner was Mr. W. H. Nelson, C.S.I. He was in the I.C.S. from 1904 till 1940, when he retired as Member of the Board of Revenue – the highest post on the land revenue side.

[37] The defence counsel was no less a person than Mr. A. K. Fazlul Huq, who became the first Prime Minister of Bengal in April 1937. That he should have appeared in a Subdivisional Magistrate's Court was most unusual, and was an indication of the public and political interest of the case.

[38] This zemindar was President of his Union Board – see Note 27. My diary records – 'When the proceedings were in camera, the Chaukidars spilt a bibful'.

[39] This school was in the south-west of the subdivision, part of the 'beel' (marsh) area, very backward in every way. The journey was made in the Madaripur Circle Officer's boat, and I did not get back to the *Rosalind* until 10.00 p.m.

[40] One factor contributing to my 'feeling an alien' was that on tour – and indeed at headquarters too – I was always accompanied by an armed bodyguard. It consisted of a couple of hairy great Pathans, who took turn and turn about on duty. The need for a bodyguard was a hangover from the Terrorist Campaign, in which Madaripur had had a bad political record.

[41] It was only with the passing of my departmental examinations in June that I had acquired 'first-class' magisterial powers, i.e. powers to impose a sentence of imprisonment up to two years. So I was very inexperienced in magisterial work when I went to Madaripur, and 'Binapani Devi v. Abdul Gafur Kotwal' was the first case of commitment to Sessions that I had ever tried. For the reasons explained in previous letters, the defence was staking everything on preventing commitment. Despite my firm belief that the case was a false one, I probably ought to have – and, with more experi-

ence, would have – committed it. Section 209(1) of the Criminal Procedure Code ran: 'When the evidence ... has been taken, and he has (if necessary) examined the accused for the purpose of enabling him to explain any circumstances appearing in the evidence against him, such Magistrate shall, if he finds that there are not sufficient grounds for committing the accused person for trial, record his reasons and discharge him ...' A standard commentary on the Code states: 'The Magistrate may weigh the evidence and if he discredits it ... he should discharge the accused. *BUT* (a) It is his duty to commit when the evidence for the prosecution is sufficient to make out a prima facie case against the accused. (b) If the question of discharge or commitment is one merely of probabilities, the Magistrate ought to leave the decision thereof to the Court of Session.'

[42] My father had been laid low with phlebitis.

[43] See Note 4.

[44] The Puja holiday was the biggest Hindu festival in the Bengali year. It lasted a fortnight, its exact incidence depending on the moon. It marked the end of the monsoon and the first hint of cooler nights, and was altogether a wonderful break. If Niranjan Bardhan had not been transferred, he, being a Hindu, would have had to have been allowed to go to his home for the Pujas, and I should have had to remain in charge.

[45] Rai Bahadur Hira Lal Moulik. The principal Indian titles 'conferred as personal distinctions by His Excellency the Viceroy' and invested by the Governor of Bengal at twice-yearly Durbars – the quotation is from an old Durbar programme – were: Rai Bahadur and Rai Sahib for Hindus; and Khan Bahadur and Khan Sahib for Muslims. One could be promoted from 'Sahib' to 'Bahadur'.

[46] 'Chaprassies' were orderlies, so called from the 'chaprash' or badge of office which they wore. The number to which one was entitled depended on one's rank: as S.D.O. I was entitled to two, and very faithful and devoted people they both were.

For 'chaukidar' see Note 27.

Section 144 of the Criminal Procedure Code dealt with injunctions, a powerful weapon in the magistrate's armoury. The side-note in the commentary mentioned in Note 41 runs: 'Power to issue order absolute at once in urgent cases of nuisance or apprehended danger.'

'Tadbir' is 'management' but colloquially it was used for all forms of string-pulling.

The A.G.B. was the Accountant-General, Bengal, and his office was (rightly) skilled at objecting to any breach of financial regulations.

D.W.s were defence witnesses.

[47] The S.D.O. had nothing to do with the Civil Courts. They were presided over by a Munsif, under the supervision of the District Judge. There was also a Munsif at Chikandi in Palong Circle – see Letter of 28 March 1937.

[48] See Note 5.

[49] It was on this occasion that we visited a High School at a char village called Sakhipura, and Mr. Hill received a very remarkable Address of Welcome. (It is referred to at the end of the Preface to the 1962 edition of *Roget's Thesaurus*: the editor of that edition was Mr. R. A. Dutch, who in 1937 became Additional District Judge of Faridpur.) Of many memorable phrases in the Address, perhaps my favourite is the description of an impoverished institution as having 'to depend entirely on income meagre and sources fungus'. The Address is reproduced in Appendix A.

[50] Sir Mirza Ismail, K.C.I.E., O.B.E. (1883–1954) was in the service of the Maharaja of Mysore from 1906 to 1926, and Dewan (Chief Minister) from 1926 to 1941.

[51] Khwaja Sir Nazimuddin, K.C.I.E. (1894–1964) was at that time one of the non-official members of the Governor's Executive Council, his portfolio being Agriculture

and Rural Development; he had previoulsy been Education Minister. Only the Home and Finance Members of the Council were officials – the seniormost members of the I.C.S. in the Province. This 'dyarchy' system of semi-responsible government in the Provinces, introduced under the Government of India Act, 1919, was shortly to give way to the Provincial autonomy of the Government of India Act, 1935. Sir Nazimuddin was a leading member of the Nawab of Dacca's family. The Nawab belonged to the old Muslim aristocracy of Mogul days, and the fact that Sir Nazimuddin spoke Urdu rather than Bengali was a political disadvantage.

[52] The Government of India Act, 1935, was due to come into force on 1 April 1937. Sir Nazimuddin was defeated for the Premiership by Mr. A. K. Fazlul Huq, but became Home Minister. He was my 'boss' for the whole of my time as Under Secretary of the Home Department from December 1937 to February 1940, and I had a great admiration for him. He was Prime Minister of Bengal from 1943 to 1945; first Prime Minister of East Pakistan in 1947; Governor-General of Pakistan from 1948 to 1951; and Prime Minister of Pakistan from 1951 to 1953.

[53] My diary tells me that this tour was mainly in Janjira police-station – where I made 'a fatuous speech' at the opening of a new dispensary. In the evening on the launch the 'jute-moths were appalling'.

25 October 1936 - 28 February 1937

Avondale, Shillong, Assam
25 October 1936

Just after posting my last letter to you, on my return from a tour on the 17th, I received a telegram from Mysore (despatched on the 13th to Rajshahi, and thus delayed) asking me to stay with the Maharaja from the 23rd till the 30th, for the annual festival of the Dashara. This was a pretty dilemma. It might have been just possible for me to get to Mysore by leaving Madaripur on the 20th (I had an unbreakable engagement on the 19th), and to stay for 4 or 5 days. This would have meant (a) being very rude to the Blanks, (b) an extremely hot, tedious & expensive railway journey, (c) an exacting programme of interesting but very formal ceremonies to witness. On the other hand, to refuse the Maharaja's invitation might mean offending him beyond repair. After much thought, I decided on Shillong, because I felt that I wanted a quiet, cool 'English' holiday more than anything else in the world. Further, as the idea behind the invitation was to see what sort of person I was, I knew that it would be difficult for me to create a favourable impression if I rushed to Mysore, worn out and unprepared, at a time when the Maharaja is fully occupied with the elaborate Dashara ceremonies. So I composed a tactful letter (not of course saying what I've said to you, but saying, with perfect truth, that I needed the sanction of Government to go to Mysore (even on a visit), and that sanction could not be obtained at a day's notice). I hope I made the right choice.

Certainly I am getting the benefit of a quiet, cool, 'English' holiday here. It was an appalling journey here. I left at 3 a.m. on the 20th, travelled by steamer for 18 hours, then by train on the night of the 20th-21st, and finally by car for 86 miles from Sylhet to Shillong, where I arrived at 5 p.m. on the 21st. The road is a comparatively new one, with the most fearsome bends and slopes. However, I had a competent Jehu, and got here none the worse.

The first three days of my holiday have not been unduly strenuous, as it's so delightful to be really lazy for a change. However, I've had one picnic lunch, one round of golf, one cabaret show, and one dance. I much enjoyed the golf; it's a lovely course. It was a pity that the Governor[54] was playing immediately behind us, so we had to hurry more than we liked. (I was playing with a guest of the Blanks' next-door neighbours, a man on the Calcutta Stock Exchange, Laver by name.) The cabaret show was very amateurish, but was quite a pleasant way of spending an evening. The dance was *most* enjoyable. It was given by the I.C.S. of Assam, and was a complete success. The Blanks gave a small dinner-party before, the other guests being from the Gurkha regiment which is stationed here. It was the first time I'd danced since May '35! Next Wednesday, I shall be going to Government House Ball.

In addition to these activities, I've brought out my flute again, and am delighted to find that, in spite of its long disuse, I could still make a tolerable noise on it. Last night Mrs. Blank and I played some Schubert songs & the familiar Handel sonatas.[55] For the rest of the time I've been catching up my arrears of private correspondence, and reading Aldous Huxley's latest novel *Eyeless in Gaza*, which is absorbing but depressing.

This morning I went to Communion. The padre here is the same nice man as was here in May '35, Boulton by name.[56] I'd like to see more of him this week, but unfortunately his children have just had measles, & his house is in quarantine.

I enclose two very bad photographs of my bungalow, and of the 'Rosalind.' The film was an old one, and the whole series has come out hopelessly underexposed, which is sad. I'll try to get some better ones on my return. . . .

I'm just off with the Blanks to Cherrapunji, the wettest place in the world (an annual rainfall of about 400 ins.!) But the sun is shining brightly and we ought to get a fine view of the Plains. Mrs. Blank sends you her best wishes.

Shillong, Assam
31 October 1936

I'm leaving this delightful place today, but before I go I must try to tell you something of the many things I have done this week. I feel a great deal better for my stay here, and, having had time to take stock of my position at Madaripur, I hope I shall in future be able to adjust my work there better. I may as well resign myself to staying there for the whole of the cold weather; Sir Mirza Ismail has just been summoned to Delhi for a conference about Federation, so probably the plan about me will be temporarily in abeyance. And in any case the negotiations about my transfer (*if* I am approved of) will have to go through the Governments of India and Bengal, which will all take time.

The only thing marring the Pujas this year has been the weather. One reckons to have finished with the rains by the end of October, but during these ten days the weather has been like Shakespeare's sonnet 'Full many a glorious morning have I seen' – fine mornings and wet afternoons. However, I've not allowed this to spoil my enjoyment of Shillong. Luckily, last Sunday was one of the few fine days, and our expedition to Cherrapunji was an unqualified success. The place did not live up to its reputation of being the wettest place in the world. We got a fine view of the plains, and had a very pleasant picnic lunch.

Monday was a comparatively quiet day. I wrote letters to a number of Cambridge friends, I had my first game of tennis for months, and I finished Aldous Huxley's latest novel, though it's almost too autobiographical to be called a novel. The chief event on Tuesday was the performance of a play of Ivor Novello by the Shillong Dramatic Society. This was quite amusing, though the action dragged. Wednesday was the night of the Government House Ball. The Blanks gave a dinner-party before. It was quite a good show, but not as enjoyable as the I.C.S. ball last week, as there were rather too many guests both for the floor and for the sitting-out accommodation; also, the programme was hurried through too quickly.

Thursday was a full day. An excellent round of golf in the morning, some tennis in the afternoon, and more amateur theatricals in the evening. This was a rival play to the A.D.S.'s production, being in aid of charities. The chief interest in it was that Mr. Blank was taking a part. He revealed an unsuspected talent for acting.

Yesterday, I watched some of the tennis tournament finals, & Mrs. Blank and I had our last bout of music together. (We've been playing a little nearly every day – the familiar old Handel sonatas, and some Schubert songs.) In the evening was the Fancy Dress Ball. We had the luck to be in the Government House party. I went as a chef, the same costume as I had worn on my last visit to Shillong. There was an excellent dinner at G.H. before, and, to my great surprise, I found myself sitting on the right of Lady Keane, who proved to be a most charming person. It was really a party for the Keanes' daughter (aged about 22, at a guess), so there were lots of young people about. The dance was held in the Club, and was a grand show. There weren't too many people, and the programme was not rushed through. Altogether, it was a very fitting climax to my holiday here.

Well, that may be a dull catalogue of events, but the holiday has not consisted simply of 'events'. Half the pleasure has been in being lazy, in having time to read, in meeting lots of friendly people, in being able to converse with people having the same cultural background. I'm quite sure I did the sensible thing in coming here, and not rushing off madly to Mysore; I told the facts to Blank, and he said that Govt. would certainly have disapproved if I'd suddenly visited Mysore in that unpremeditated fashion. . . .

Time to go out and do some final shopping before my departure.

Madaripur, East Bengal
8 November 1936

I've missed the week-end air-mail, I'm afraid, but I'll start this letter now and finish it on Tuesday, by which time your latest letters ought to have arrived. I'm glad to be able to report slight progress in the Mysore matter. I had a letter a few days ago from H.H.'s Private Secretary, a man with the delightful name of Thumboo Chetty, asking me on what terms I would accept the appointment if H.H. were to offer it. So I wrote back today, mentioning among other things that I was intending to take leave in the spring of 1938. It was a bit difficult knowing what to suggest by way of pay, being given carte blanche in this way. I am drawing Rs.700/- per month now, plus Rs.70/- or 80/- travelling allowance, but my expeness there would be higher, so I suggested Rs.1000/- per month.[57]

I had a much nicer journey back from Shillong than the journey there. I had some nice travelling companions in the shape of a Mr. & Mrs. Stuart;[58] he was acting as District Magistrate of Dacca, but very young for such a big post. She was charming. . . .

This week's work has been much more pleasant than usual, partly because I'm feeling mentally refreshed, partly because I've determined that I'm jolly well not going to overwork myself, and partly because the nights have begun to cool down. Indeed the mornings have quite a nip in the air, which I was not expecting to feel till the end of the month. I'm beginning to concentrate on election matters. The polling of the primary elections of the Depressed Classes (= outcastes) is being held on November 21st, but I'm not a 'Returning Officer', so my responsibility will not be great. But in the final elections, I am the Returning Officer for two Constituencies,[59] which means that I shall have to accept & scrutinize candidates' nomination papers before the polling, and count the votes after. As the majority of the electorate is illiterate, a new system of voting is being tried, with the use of symbols,[60] so that instead of voting for Abdul Karim you vote for an umbrella, and instead of Subodh Chandra Chatterji you vote for a mango-tree. We have recently received more than 200 ballot-boxes each about the size of a cider-barrel, which will all have to be plastered with these symbols. Long live Democracy! (Incidentally, democracy did score a startlingly big victory in the States; Governor Landon must be feeling a worm and no man.)[61]

Yesterday, I had quite a change of work, in particpating in a water-hyacinth[62] demonstration. (Do you remember I did some of this work at Rajshahi in the early part of 1935?) The site had been badly selected, but we did quite a lot of hard work, and I got filthily dirty from head to foot, which had very good propaganda value! I'm going out tomorrow again, and being called at 4.45 a.m., so I think I'll go to bed now.

9 November 1936

I got back earlier than I expected today, and found your latest letters awaiting me ... I'm sorry to hear that the tree which used to support the old swing has fallen down; – one more change to notice when I return; the chief change will be the electric light. I can't really visualize Waldershare with electric light. Here, of course, I have no such luxury, having to be content with petrol lamps,[63] which however give a very bright light ...

I received the Autumn Books number of the *New Statesman*, & I look forward to reading it. But at the same time, I think I must ask you to stop sending me the *N.S.* from now on. It's really impossible and undesirable for a member of the I.C.S. (particularly if he goes to a Native State) to be an enthusiastic and regular reader of the *N.S.*, as I am at present!

Madaripur, East Bengal
14 November 1936

As I wrote as recently as Monday, there's not a great deal to report today, but I know you like me to write by the week-end rather than the mid-week mail, so here goes.

I paid my first visit to Palong on the 11th and 12th. This is the most important place in my subdivision, but I purposely didn't go there during my first three months here, while the big abduction case was pending in my court. I held a number of meetings, and also organized yet another water-hyacinth demonstration. Our work was quite effective, in spite of an inadequate response by the local non-officials. But as I had felt slight suspicions of a cold coming the previous day, and as the work entailed wading and swimming through mud and water for more than two hours, the result was that I came back with a first-class 'streamer'. Luckily yesterday and today were holidays in honour of the Kali Puja, so I have not had to go to Court. Yesterday I felt pretty miserable, but today I'm much better, & by tomorrow I know I'll be fit again.

The Boyles came to lunch today. They gave me some helpful advice about my garden. My vegetables, especially the beans, are coming on nicely, but the flowers are so far a little disappointing. I've got beans & peas, cabbage, cauliflower, tomatoes, beetroot, lettuce & radishes all coming up quite well, but I suppose it will be another month before I'm eating my own vegetables.

My leisure has given me an opportunity to use my gramaphone more than before. My three albums of the 'Columbia History of Music' were certainly a good investment.

I'm going over to Char Mugria tomorrow evening for dinner and Mah Jong with the Boyles. They tell me that one of the Charmugria jute-wallahs has a new wireless on which they all heard the Cenotaph service perfectly on the 11th, I wish I'd been able to be there. . . .

Madaripur, East Bengal
21 November 1936

I've been at headquarters all this week, and the criminal work has been very heavy. This is the paddy-harvesting season, which always produces a crop of broken heads and boundary disputes. In the last 5 days I must have heard between 60 and 70 complaint petitions. Of course a lot of these will be compromised. On Wednesday we had a conference of all the presiding and polling officers of the 23 polling centres in this subdivision, and I tried to explain to them the elaborate new procedure of voting by the symbol system. Today I've got a respite, as it's polling day for the Scheduled Castes (= outcastes) and as all the other magistrates and the clerks are presiding & polling officers, the office here is closed and it's a holiday. I've spent most of it poring over the blue prints for the new subdivisional headquarters, and writing out a list of suggested improvements.

I don't think I shall be there to see the new headquarters. On Thursday morning, I got a wire from the Maharaja's Sceretary which I will quote in full. 'Thanks for your letter. Your appointment will be for one year on Rs.1000/- per month with free house and travelling allowance at rates allowed to Deputy Commissioners here. You will maintain your own car. Palace makes food and other arrangements when travelling with Prince. Your duties will principally be supervision of games, riding exercises, shooting, travelling with Prince, moving in society and be helpful generally. Could you kindly come to Bangalore for a couple of days before the end of this month? We will pay first class railway fare to and fro; wire reply.' Of course it was impossible even to contemplate dashing off to Bangalore at a moment's notice at a time which is not a public holiday, and they ought to have known that any member of the I.C.S. can't leave his station without getting leave, and can't get leave without giving some warning. So I wired back 'Regret quite impossible to get leave to come to Bangalore this month. With your approval will negotiate for leave during last week of December. Please wire reply.' So I hope to go for an 'interview' at Christmas, and if they like the look of me, I'll try to get transferred from here by February. They seem to be pretty keen to get hold of me, and Rs.1000/- is princely pay, though I expect my expenses will be high too. The duties sound a bit ominous, though, and when they find that I am neither a Blue, nor a brilliant horseman, nor an experienced shikari, nor a bridge-player, they may think twice about offering the appointment to me. However, I think that they may have included in the wire only the sides of the work that they thought would be most attractive to me, making the assumption (completely false nowadays) that people in the I.C.S. have ample leisure and opportunity for such sporting activities. However, I hope if I go there for Christmas I shall be able to cut a decent figure. It sounds as if they wanted a hearty Conservative, rather than an intellectual Liberal (a rather ghastly description of me, but you know what I mean). Can the leopard change his spots? Should he try?

If I write any longer I'll miss the mail. Also, my Mahommedan peon, who will take the letter to the post, has been fasting all day as it's the month of Ramazan, and now that the sun is setting he wants to break his fast.

as from Madaripur, East Bengal
28 November 1936

I am writing today from Faridpur, the occasion being, as usual, the District Board meeting. It is an unusually important one this month, as a new District Engineer is to be chosen; there are 47 candidates, and the amount of canvassing & wire-pulling that has been going on is enormous. There are only 3 Moslem candidates, but they stand a better chance than their 44 Hindu competitors, many of whom are better qualified, as the majority of the D.B. members are Moslems. You have no idea of the way that the communal feeling penetrates into every nook & cranny of public & private life here.

Last Sunday I was asked to preside at a meeting of the Ramkrishna Centenary Celebrations, one of the Swamis from the Ramkrishna Mission being the chief speaker. I hastily read Romain Rolland's life of Ramkrishna before, & was expecting quite an interesting meeting, but actually the Swami, though he had a very saintly appearance, read an address just like an ordinary tub-thumping demagogue. Monday & Tuesday were both public holidays (we've been having a galaxy of them lately), so I got through quite a lot of useful work. On Wednesday I had meant to go on tour to inspect a High School and a Union Board, but the previous day Hafizuddin came with news of a big Moslem gathering where there might be a breach of the peace, & he wanted me to go with him. There are two Moslem factions here, one the Jumma party & the other the non-Jumma party; the former say congregational prayers on Friday & the latter don't. Feeling runs high on the point. An argument between two influential men of each party had been arranged, but it frequently happens in these meetings that the party which is worsted by words will resort to blows, so we took the precaution of bringing a body of armed police. But eventually the leader of the non-Jumma party failed to turn up, & boycotted the meeting. So it was attended by less than a thousand people, & was all very peaceful and unanimous. But it was quite an interesting day, & useful experience; and it certainly wasn't worth taking the risk of a riot.

I have received a definite invitation to come to Mysore just after Christmas, so I shall apply for a few days leave to tack on to the Christmas holidays.

I'm staying at the Collector's Bungalow as usual. Mrs. Hill is here. I only saw her for about an hour after my arrival late yesterday evening. She is very engrossed in her son, aged one. It's time for breakfast, so – –

as from Madaripur, East Bengal
5 December 1936

I am writing this week from Bhedarganj, where I have come to renew gun-licences. I am making a tour of all the thanas this fortnight to do this work ,with which I am very familiar from my previous experience at Rajshahi.[64] It is a great comfort to have the 'Rosalind' back again. She is very spick and span after her annual overhaul, and she can travel faster too. Several minor improvements have been made, e.g. shelves in the cabin, & a small fan in the bathroom.

. . . It was nice of Mrs. Blank to write to you; having her daughters at home, she fully realizes how much you appreciate any first-hand news of me. . . . .

I wrote last from Faridpur. The journey back from there was amazingly tedious; it took 24 hours, mostly in a revolting little paddle-steamer with a revolving paddle at the back which looked like an egg-whisk. Things will be worse still in January & February, as the Palong river, which is the main communication with the outside world, practically dries up. On my return, I had three busy days at headquarters, and then started on my present tour.

I have applied for 4 days' leave to be affixed to the Christmas holidays to enable me to get to Mysore. It takes an awful long time to get there, but all the travelling will be by night, and I shall have days in Calcutta and Madras both ways. I hope my leave will be sanctioned.

There is no more news, and this is the last page of my air-mail block.

P.S. A 7-lb. chest of Lopchu tea ought to be arriving for you pretty soon. It was sent off from Darjeeling on the 21st.

Madaripur, East Bengal
13 December 1936

When I wrote only a week ago, I had no suspicion that a constitutional crisis was even impending. And now we have a new King and Queen on the Throne. The speed with which the events have taken place is surprising, though those who read the cheap American press must have been talking for a long time. The loss to the Empire is a very great one, for the character of the Prince of Wales had gripped the people's imagination and affection in a way that the Duke of York's never had. But to have a person like Mrs. Simpson as Queen was absolutely out of the question. What an unhappy business.

I know at the time of the Duke of York's marriage we worked out the exact relationship between ourselves and Lady Elizabeth Bowes-Lyon, but I can't remember exactly which of my ancestors it was that married into the Strathmore family.[65]

I've not got much news of my own to contribute. I've been on tour half the week renewing gun-licences. On my way back on Friday evening, I was passing through Charmugria, and I dropped in on Stansbury, an old jute-merchant, to hear his wireless which is a very good set. I heard the special Empire news, which contained the reproduction of Baldwin's speech, and the news of the passing of the Abdication Bill. It made me feel very close in touch with England, and I was glad I had the opportunity to listen.[66]

I am definitely getting leave to go to Mysore. Most of the holiday will be spent in travelling to and fro, but most of the journeys are by night, and I shall have days in Calcutta and Madras both ways. I have not yet told the authorities here of my possible appointment in Mysore, in case the coming interview has an unfavourable result.

I heard today that Hill is going to visit Madaripur tomorrow. I don't know what he's coming for, but I wish he'd give longer notice, as his visits dislocate my work completely. However, there are several things I wanted to see him about personally before Christmas, so I'm quite glad in one way.

14 December 1936

Your latest letters came this morning, and I've just time to scribble a hasty reply... Father's comments on the Crisis were most interesting to read in the light of subsequent developments.... Some questions to answer – I keep up a regular correspondence with John Pilcher[67] in Tokyo; I never by any chance see the *London Mercury*; and my bread is from the bazaar – quite tasteless.

Madaripur, East Bengal
20 December 1936

There's not much news to interest you this week, I'm afraid. Tuesday and Wednesday were holidays for the big Mahommedan festival, the Id-ul-Fitr, which is the equivalent of Christmas.... On Wednesday I went to dine with the Boyles at Charmugria, combined with the usual game of Mah Jong. For the first time I walked both ways.[68] It's 3/4 of an hour each way, which prevents me going very often.

Election fever is rising. I have been receiving nomination papers during the past week for the two constituencies of which I am in charge, and yesterday was fixed for the scrutiny of nomination papers. There are two candidates in the East Mahommedan constituency, and four in the West. Some of the latter may withdraw, if they receive sufficient financial inducement. The amount of dirty work behind the scenes, of which I get occasional glimpses, is something incredible. In the West constituency, there is one very wealthy candidate, the nephew of an influential but bankrupt & debauched zemindar; he resides in Jalpaiguri, and may be able to get the seat with the help of his long purse. The other three are all local men, who are all so jealous of each other that they won't stand down in favour of the other.[69] They all pretend to represent the 'proja' party ('proja' = tenant), but really they are only out for their own interest, as is shown by their refusal to combine against the zemindar's candidate.

I have been skimming rapidly through Jawaharlal Nehru's autobiography. I should have liked to read it thoroughly, but it's a very big volume. I don't know if you read it when it came out early this year. It's a very bitter indictment of the British Government in India, and that is scarcely surprising from a man who has been kept in prison half the time since the War for political reasons. We have much to answer for, but certainly not all that Jawaharlal imputes to us.

I am writing on the 'Rosalind' on the way back from a committee meeting about the re-excavation of a long canal in Palong circle. It will be of great benefit if it is made navigable throughout the year. There is some opposition, as is inevitable when extra taxes are imposed,[70] but we're pushing the scheme through. The work is to start in February. I'm beginning to get quite interested in the subdivision, now that I know it better, and even if I don't get the Mysore job, I shall be resigned to staying here, at any rate till the Rains....

as from Madaripur, East Bengal
Boxing Day, 1936

I am writing this week from a hotel in Madras. I leave for Mysore this evening. It has been a very un-Christmassy Christmas for me this year. I was hard at work at Madaripur till the 23rd, on the afternoon of which I left for Calcutta. The steamer journey to Khulna was very slow, crowded and uncomfortable. There were only two cabins, one of which was occupied by the leading member of the Madaripur Bar[71] and his wife, and the other was shared by my third officer, Mukerjee,[72] and myself. There was rather a crisis when, at an intermediate station, a lady missionary embarked. She was, I think, a Scandinavian, and she was a Seventh Day Adventist into the bargain. The saloon was already stuffed with people, so she slept in the pantry. If it had been any season but the cold weather,

Mukerjee and I might have given up our cabin and slept on deck, but my chivalrous instincts were not sufficiently strong to make me want to court pneumonia. And the pantry looked quite snug!

I had a pretty full day in Calcutta on Christmas Eve. My wardrobe needed a bit of supplementing before I could face a Maharajah. I'd ordered a new suit by post, and I had a first fitting as soon as I arrived. The suit was ready for me to take away that evening; Indian tailors can work quickly. I also bought a new wrist-watch,[73] as my old one was growing very erratic. The only snag in the day's programme was that Grindlay's had failed to send my tickets to the U.S. Club, and, as they were closed for Christmas Eve, I had to buy myself tickets anew. Fortunately I had enough cash in hand to do this, but it may mean running a bit short here.

The journey from Calcutta to Madras was interesting in a mild way, but the country is not very exciting anywhere. It took 38 hours – 2 nights and a day. In places, we were within sight of the Eastern Ghats, which rise very suddenly from the paddy-field plains; the formation looked volcanic. I was principally interested in seeing the differences of agriculture, architecture & dress of the Madras peasant from the Bengal peasant. Small-scale irrigation is in evidence everywhere here, for Nature has not given such a generous river system here as in Bengal. The villages seemed to be more compact units than in Bengal, where a village is merely an arbitrary collection of isolated homesteads.

I don't know a soul in Madras, so today is being rather tedious, especially as it's Boxing Day and everything is shut. Perhaps I'm being rather unenterprising not sightseeing, but there's nothing wildly exciting in the town itself, and anyway sightseeing's a dull game alone. I've just finished an exceedingly good lunch, and it's too hot to go out. After a month of European clothes in Bengal, I'm back into white trousers and a thin coat – and glad of a fan above my head. Mysore, however, will be distinctly cooler.

Well, this week will settle my fate one way or the other. Probably my next letter will be a long one. Thank you for the genealogical tree showing our connection with the Queen.

as from Madaripur, East Bengal
3 January 1937

I shall be going to Mysore. I'll tell you the whole story later in the letter. I did not get your letter suggesting a cable until I arrived here, and in these days of rapid Air Mail it really didn't seem cable-worthy.

I wrote last the day before my arrival in Mysore. I got there at 11.0 on the 27th and was met by the Superintendent of Guests, who drove me off to my guest-house, a nice bungalow on the outskirts of the town. On the way there, I could see what a fine town it was, spacious streets, good buildings, and abundant flowers. Town-planning is one of Sir Mirza Ismail's hobbies. That afternoon, I rested after lunch – a habit which is supposed to be universal in India, but in which I haven't indulged for months; then I had a round of golf on a small but entertaining course with Major Nabi Khan, an A.D.C., and Dr. Robinson, the Palace Surgeon. The next item on the programme was Evensong at the English Church with Lady Todhunter, the wife of the Private Secretary. It was a pleasant surprise to be able to go to church and hear a few Christmas hymns, and quite a good sermon from the chaplain of Bangalore. I then dined with the Todhunters. Sir Charles is retired from the Civil Service in Madras, now well on in life but very active and a great worker. He is *Private* Secretary, & his job is to put up all the Government stuff to the Maharaja – i.e. he is the liaison between the Palace at Mysore and the Administration at Bangalore. He is not to be confused with Mr. Thumboo Chetty, the *Huzur* Secretary, who is simply concerned with Palace affairs, and with whom I have been corresponding. After dinner, I was driven out to see the Krishnarajsagar Dam, across the river Cauvery, which is one of the biggest dams in India. It has as a side-show an ornamental garden with fountains, which are lit by coloured lights by night. The *tout ensemble* was quite effective. Sir Mirza Ismail's work again.

The next day I got down to business, and saw Thumboo Chetty. He was polite but non-committal. He is a devout Roman Catholic. I then paid a number of calls, the most interesting of which was on a Mr. & Mrs. Rollo. He is Principal of the Maharaja's College in the Mysore University, and told me lots about Prince Jaya, of whose studies he now has the care. Jaya had unfortunately just started on a long trip to Bombay, Delhi and Agra. This was bad management, as he could have easily waited a couple of days to see me; 'Hamlet without the Prince' with a vengeance. He fired me with enthusiasm for the job, for Jaya is at a critical age, and torn between good and bad influences. Jaya is a good pianist and fond of music, like the rest of his family.

I lunched with Major Khan, who has a very pretty English wife (but born and brought up in India, I think). In the afternoon I had a brief audience with the Maharaja. A man small in stature but great in all other respects. I think he liked the look of me, for the next morning Thumboo Chetty told me the matter had been decided in my favour. I was then taken for a little more sight-seeing by the Superintendent. I was to have dined at the Palace that evening, but I had to excuse myself as I was suddenly seized with an internal upset. This has been with me ever since.

I had a most miserable night on the 28th, and on the 29th I stayed in bed most of the morning. However, I managed to see Chetty & talk over some details with him. It was decided that I must go to Bangalore, and we left that afternoon by train. On arrival I went straight to a comfortable hotel and bed. My time was much beguiled by Robert Graves' excellent novel *I, Claudius*, which I had not read when it came out; I look forward to reading the sequel, *Claudius the God*. I am only surprised that the Roman Empire didn't decline and fall long before it did!

On the 30th, I saw Prince Jaya's father, the Yuvaraja, and also Sir Mirza Ismail. Then I called at the Residency, but Col. Plowden was away. However, I saw his Personal Assistant, & told him about the appointment. The correspondence will have to go through the Residency.

I left Bangalore on the morning of my birthday, and spent the afternoon writing letters in the waiting-room of Madras station, as I didn't feel fit to do any sight-seeing. Then came the tedious journey back to Calcutta, rendered all the more tedious because I couldn't appreciate the ordinarily palatable meals provided in the Restaurant car. By the way, my indisposition prevented me taking a lot of photographs at Mysore. However, as I'll be returning there, I'll have ample opportunity later.

I arrived here yesterday morning to find a huge mail awaiting me. I spent a rather fruitless afternoon, as I found to my disgust that all the big shops were shut as it was a Saturday. I had meant to buy a gun at Manton's. I went to see Carritt,[74] and learnt to my relief that there'd be no objection on the part of the Bengal Government to my going to Mysore. That was the last hurdle cleared. (I learnt incidentally that I was in the running for succeeding to Carritt's job of Political Under Secretary. This is an extremely hardworked job, but a 'step to higher things', as it brings one in contact with all the bigwigs of Government. One also lives in Calcutta and Darjeeling. As I'm going to Mysore, the job will probably go to Kitchin, who will enjoy it much more than I should have.)

Today I managed to get to the Cathedral early. I'm lunching with the Hendersons, and then I must be off to Madaripur, where I hope plain and regular meals will put my inside right again.

I'll let you know my Mysore address as soon as I know it myself. You can start sending me the *New Statesman* again.

Madaripur, East Bengal
12 January 1937

I was so glad to get the letters you wrote on my birthday. You seem to have had a happy though quiet Christmas. I'm glad the chest of tea arrived safely.

There's not much news to give you since my return from Calcutta. I've got so absorbed into Madaripur affairs again, that the visit to Mysore seems almost like a dream, and I can hardly believe that I shall be going there in a month or so. I have kept my departure a strict secret[75] here, as it would have a very bad effect on the administration of the subdivision if the people knew I was due for a move. I've only told Hafizuddin. I'm writing this on board the 'Rosalind', on my way to Faridpur once again, and I shall take the opportunity of telling Hill about Mysore. The occasion of this visit is, as usual, a District Board meeting, but today is fixed for the last meeting of the old Board, and tomorrow for the Election to the Chairmanship of the new Board. It is going to be a very fierce struggle between a man of my subdivision and a man of Faridpur.[76] For the last month the two candidates have been rushing about canvassing for the votes of the 30 members; I hold a rather key position, as I can influence the votes of most of the men of my subdivision. Lobbying is quite an amusing game, but it's played too much in Bengal.

My tummy trouble persisted for several days after my return to Madaripur, but I'm thankful to say that my inside has at last returned to practically normal conditions. The work has not been excessively heavy, and I've only been out on tour for one day. I've had time to read *Claudius the God* which I much enjoyed.

Madaripur, East Bengal
17 January 1937

. . . My trip to Faridpur was much the most pleasant yet. The 'Rosalind' arrived at noon on the 12th, and we drove six miles in to the town on a perfectly appalling road in a very dilapidated taxi. That afternoon was occupied by the last meeting of the old District Board. In the evening Doha gave a dinner-party to all the assembled officials and their wives. The next morning was spent in work of one sort or another, and then came the momentous District Board Chairmanship Election. Actually, the whole thing had been settled in the secret meetings which had been held the previous night, but even so the atmosphere was very tense. Luckily we got the room clear of the public, who were surging round on all sides, When the votes were counted, the Madaripur candidate (the Chairman of the last Board) was defeated by 22 votes to 6. I wasn't really sorry, because his rival is undoubtedly a more able and a more honest man, who got the support of all the men of Madaripur except two. We had the additional compensation of getting the Vice-Chairman. The members of the new Board seem on the whole to be much more able than their predecessors, and I hope the new brooms will sweep clean – there's plenty of dust to sweep away, for the old Board was pretty corrupt.

That evening Hafizuddin and I went to the cinema & saw the best Bengali film I've yet seen, called *Maya*. When I leave this place, Hafizuddin will be one of the few people I shall be really sorry to say Good-bye to; we understand each other singularly well. It's been an enormous help to the administration of this subdivision. In the past there have been instances of the S.D.O. & the S.D.P.O. not getting on well together, and the public take full advantage of the situation.

On the 15th I went with Hafizuddin and a Captain S— to preside over the Sports Meeting of the East Madaripur Inter-School Association. S— is a new Military Intelligence Officer; he didn't strike me as being either very military or very intelligent, but he was a great help that day. The meeting was an unqualified success. Everything went off smoothly, and the standard of the competitors was quite high. I presented a cup to the winning school team, which I'd bought on my way through Calcutta. There'll be a similar meeting here on next Sunday, for the High Schools of West Madaripur. Each association will send a team to Faridpur to contest in the District Sports, which are going to be held on February 7th. I shall go, as the District Board Meeting has been arranged on the 6th. I hope that will be my last visit to Faridpur.

The Provincial Legislative Assembly election is now upon us. All my officers and nearly all my clerks[77] have left for their respective polling centres. The office will be practically closed for the whole of this week. I was expecting to have quite a holiday, but now I find I shall really have a good deal to do. Also, I'll have to be ready to dash off anywhere if there is a disturbance. The most likely quarter for trouble is Sibchar police station, where the ex-Chairman of the District Board is a candidate; if the voting is strongly against him, he may try to resort to force.

Madaripur, East Bengal
23 January 1937

I'm taking advantage of a holiday to catch the week-end Air Mail. If I wait till your letters come, I shall have to write a scrambled letter, as I shall be frantically busy next week. This week has been quite unlike any other that I've spent in Madaripur. It has been a holiday in the sense that the office has been closed on account of the elections. All my officers have gone out to the mofussil to act as Presiding Officers and all the clerks except 6, a mere skeleton staff to keep the work going. This has meant that I have had to hold the fort alone, and do all the work that was to be done. For there is a certain amount of indispensable daily routine work – the opening and reading of the 'dak', the sending of arrested accused persons to jail, hearing criminal complaints, doing a few Treasury[78] transactions, etc etc. Apart from that, I have had to type my own confidential letters, and I very much miss my nice Confidential Clerk. One does come to rely on a 'private secretary'. I have managed to get through quite a lot of useful work, making preparations for the Inter-School Sports of West Madaripur which are to be held tomorrow, arranging for the counting of votes on the 26th and 27th, & clearing off a lot of judicial and other files which had fallen into arrears.

Then there was the election going on all the time, with last minute telegrams coming in about polling officers falling ill, express letters from candidates saying that there would be a riot at such and such a polling centre & could they please have an extra police force. We were expecting trouble from Sibchar P.S. and were fully prepared to go there in the launch, but everything went off peacefully. On the 21st, the second day for Mahommedan polling, Hafizuddin & I did actually make a short trip to one polling centre where we thought feelings might run rather high.

The polling centre was situated very near the house of a zemindar of ancient family, whose nephew is one of the candidates. The rival candidate had decided to be present to see that the zemindar did not exercise undue influence on the voters, who were mostly his tenants. We got there in the afternoon about an hour before the polling was due to stop, but found everything quite peaceful. There was a big crowd, as the zemindar had cunningly given orders that the bazaar which is usually held two miles away should be held near the polling-station that day. One candidate had as his Symbol an umbrella, and the other a hurricane-lamp, and their canvassers were rushing about waving specimens of these symbols, seizing any voter who had not cast his vote, and pushing him towards the pooling booth. It was quite a picturesque scene, and I wished I had brought my camera with me.

It sounds from all this as if I'd been pretty busy, but actually I've had more leisure than usual. On Monday, I spent a long evening with the Boyles, playing Mah Jong and talking nineteen to the dozen as usual. On Wednesday, the Dohas suddenly came by launch from Faridpur, so I asked them to tea. Mrs. Doha was in strict purdah until her marriage, but is now completely emancipated. The next day the Hafizuddins gave a lunch-party for them. Yesterday, I had the Hafizuddins to lunch. Mrs. H. is still in semi-purdah, and can hardly talk any English; she's a pretty little person. After lunch I took a photograph of them. I hope it will come out well,[79] for without the Hafizuddins (and the Boyles) I could scarcely have tolerated Madaripur.

Last night I got out my flute for the first time since Shillong, and was pleased to find myself not too out of practice. I'm in the middle of a most interesting book called *The Decline and Fall of the Romantic Ideal* by F. L. Lucas, sent to me as a Christmas present by my Wykehamist friend John Cole.

On board the S.L. 'Rosalind', Madaripur, Bengal
31 January 1937

... Your latest letters just reached me this evening. ... You have asked several questions about Mysore which I shall answer one by one. (1) I don't know yet who will succeed me, but I don't envy him! (2) Hedayet Ali did come with me to Mysore, and may come with me again, but I doubt if he'd stay there for long away from his own people. (3) I probably shan't have to learn any new language. English is very widely known, and Hindustani will carry me through in some other places. Kanarese is the vernacular of Mysore, a language allied to Tamil & Telegu. (4) I shall have nothing to do with Prince Jaya's studies officially, but I shall do what I can to help him in a general way, as far as my own knowledge permits. (5) I think there is a Chaplain at Mysore, but he was away when I was there. (6) I shall be paid from the Palace Treasury, so the Bengal Govt. will save my screw. I'm getting Rs.700/- a month here (of which I save about half), and I shall get Rs.1000/- a month there. This should be sufficient to cover the much higher standard of living I shall have to adopt e.g. keeping a car, entertainment expenses, club bills etc etc. But I shall get a free house.

The last week has been a *very* heavy week's work – just like the bad old days of August and September. On Sunday the 24th the Inter School Sports were held at Madaripur. I'd managed to get the preparations made fairly efficiently, but I hadn't got such a good band of helpers as at Upashi the week before. However, all went off quite well. Tuesday and Wednesday were the days fixed for counting the votes in the General Election. I'm glad to say that my plans for counting went off very smoothly & I was able to get the job done much earlier than I expected. In East Madaripur, an aristocratic landowner defeated a proletarian by 8500 to 6500, and in West Madaripur, a pleader defeated a zemindar by 5500 to 5000 votes.[80] The elections all over Bengal have been an absorbing topic of conversation, but these politics would be of no interest to you. Monday, Thursday & Friday were hectically busy days, with a stream of visitors each morning, heavy accumulations of work at office, and meetings each evening.

I escaped on tour yesterday, but that's not been a rest cure either. Yesterday I inspected a Union Board and 3 schools, settled a dispute about a latrine, and attended a Hindu wedding dinner-party. (Unfortunately I saw nothing of the wedding itself.) Today I have seen two projected roads, and presided over two public meetings. Inspecting the contemplated route of the roads has meant walking 8 or 9 miles, which I have never had the chance to do in Madaripur before. It's 10.15 now and I'm quite ready for bed.

P.S. I got a letter today asking me to fill up the routine form of application for work in the Foreign & Political Department; I think this means that things are moving in Delhi at last.

Madaripur, East Bengal
8 February 1937

I'm writing this on board the 'Rosalind', so my writing may joggle a bit from the throbbing of the engine. I'm on my way back from one of my monthly trips to Faridpur. This time for the first time Mrs. Hafizuddin and the baby have come too. We travelled on the 5th day, arriving at Faridpur just after sunset. The baby daughter is just over a year old, and is a nice cheerful little creature, named Mina. She has behaved very well on the launch.

I had three very busy days at headquarters on the 2nd, 3rd & 4th. On the 2nd evening, the richest jute merchant of Charmugria gave a tea-party in my honour to all the leading people of Madaripur and Charmugria. It was quite a successful function, but the motive behind it – nothing is ever done here without a motive – was in connection with the nominated members for the Municipality. The elected members are such a rotten lot of uneducated people that I shall have to be very careful about who I nominate,[81] if the Municipality is not to make a complete hash of the transfer of the subdivisional headquarters.

The trip to Faridpur was a very enjoyable change. On the night I arrived, the Hills and I went to the theatre! There isn't a permanent theatre in Faridpur, but a special company of very talented actors had come from Calcutta for 5 days, with a different play each night. We saw one of Tagore's plays. It was inordinately long (7 till 12.30), but well worth seeing; it's the first proper Bengali play I've seen. The actors spoke their lines beautifully clearly. The theme was the struggle between the orthodox Hindus and the Brahmo Samaj,[82] & one really needed to be a Hindu to appreciate it.

The 6th was mainly occupied by the District Board meeting. The members of the new Board are much abler than those of the old, and the Chairman is a great improvement. Yesterday was the day fixed for the District Inter-School Sports. It was a much hotter day than we've had before, and from now on the thermometer will begin to rise steadily. The Sports went off well, and the Madaripur teams acquitted themselves quite creditably. I had taken a lot of trouble about this matter.

I'm at last beginning to grow really impatient about my move to Mysore. The wheels of Government move so infernally slowly that I probably won't get away much before March. It's difficult to be really enthusiastic about work of which one will not see the results, or which one will have to leave half-done....

On my arrival at Madaripur I found a letter from Thumboo Chetty saying that Prince Jaya is contemplating a trip to China & Japan from April to June, & asking me to go too. The itinerary is – Leave Mysore on the 1st April, & reach Singapore on 4th. Stay there till the 10th. Thence to Tokyo via Shanghai. 3 weeks in Tokyo, 1 week in Yokohama, 1 week in Kyoto. Isn't it too sickening that I shall get to Singapore just after Margaret's and Ronald's departure. But it's an exciting prospect. John Pilcher will be a godsend in Tokyo. All this is an additional reason for me to leave early, so that I may get to know Prince Jaya a little before making such a momentous journey with him.

Madaripur, East Bengal
14 February 1937

One item of news overshadows everything else. On the 10th I received an unofficial note from Carritt saying that Government had decided that they could not spare my services for the Mysore job.

This was a most unpleasant surprise, as Carritt had told me, when I saw him in Calcutta in January, that he was sure that there could be no objection if the Govt. of Mysore through the Govt. of India asked for my services by name. I wrote at once to Thumboo Chetty, and also to Carritt to ask for copies of the letters to & from the Govt. of India, so that I may know just who has objected and why; then I will know what sort of representation to make against this infuriating decision. By an ironic coincidence, two very nice letters of congratulation came from the Bartons by the same post, and Sir William mentioned incidentally that he'd heard from B. J. Glancy,[88] the Foreign Secy. at Delhi, that there'd be no difficulty as far as he was concerned. It's ridiculous for the Govt. of Bengal to pretend that somebody so junior as I am is in the least indispensable, especially when it's only a temporary job.

You may be thinking that I should have got the Govt. of Bengal's consent before entering into any negotiations with Mysore at all. But to begin with, Sir William's first letter said that 'the Govt. of Bengal might not want to lose you, but they could hardly object'. Secondly, it would have been very imprudent of me to mention to the Govt. of Bengal that I was trying to escape from the Province until a definite offer was made to me, and it was not until I'd been to Mysore that such an offer was made. Well, I've done all I can for the moment, and it's no use worrying. Now that the cat *is* out of the bag, I shan't let the matter drop easily. In the meantime, I must just carry on with the work here, though I can't pretend that I am doing that with much zeal or grace.

You are probably as bored of hearing of my activities at Madaripur as I am bored of doing them, but I may mention that I've been out on tour most of this week. This morning I had my first shooting of the season, after duck with Hafizuddin, on the way back from a tour. These teal fly about in huge flocks, and if you can get close enough to them before they get up, one can blaze away 'into the brown' with a certainty of bringing down a few. Our 'bag' this morning will provide me with dinner tonight, which I am giving to the Hills. They have also been touring, and are passing through Madaripur en route for Faridpur. I've had to organize a Water Hyacinth Demonstration for his benefit tomorrow; I hope that all will go well; I left the details to my Circle Officer[84] who's a lazy and unreliable cove.

I had a cold on the 8th & 9th, but got rid of it pretty quickly. There's no more news – but the first two pages are enough to keep you thinking!

16 Feburary 1937

Your letters of the 5th came this morning, and I may reply to some points at once.... I have just written a long letter in answer to a *most* interesting letter from David Barclay Baron,[85] frankly advising him not to come into the I.C.S. He's of a very Labour turn of mind, I believe. The enigma of the I.C.S. at present is that a Conservative would hate having to treat Indians as equals or superiors, and a Labourite would hate being unable to put his political principles into practice, & being the sort of little tin god I am here! *The Times* is very misleading about the real conditions of the I.C.S....

I got another note from Carritt yesterday, saying that there was *no* correspondence with the Govt. of India. The Govt. of Bengal was 'merely asked by Mysore whether we would be prepared to let you go if the Govt. of India approved & our reply to that was in the negative'. Carritt further added 'I am sorry if I misled you when I saw you in Calcutta, but of course that could only be my personal opinion.' So there doesn't seem to be much ground for hope, unless Mysore chooses to make itself nasty.

Madaripur, East Bengal
22 February 1937

There is no development in the Mysore situation, but I am expecting a letter from Mysore any day. Candidly, though, I have not much hope of being allowed to go. The time-lag of the air-mail is rather tantalizing, as each of your letters brings news of more congratulations on my appointment – alas illusory.

Today I have eaten beef[86] for the first time for many months. This is because the festival of Id-uz-zuha or Bakr-Id occurred today, on which cows are sacrificed. I am glad to say that no report of communal trouble has come to my ears. The Hindus are apt to be enraged if they see the cows slaughtered. Talking of communal trouble, the Abduction Case which filled so much of my time and thoughts during the first 2½ months of my time in Madaripur is at long last going to be tried by the Sessions Court at Faridpur. The accused have tried to get the case transferred elsewhere by the High Court, but without success. There is a chance that the Sessions Judge, who is a Hindu, will transfer the case to the new Assistant Sessions Judge, an Englishman called Dutch,[87] who has just arrived. But I'm afraid he'll insist on trying it himself, in which case it's 10 to 1 that the accused will be convicted, even though I *know* that the case is a completely false one.

I have again been out on tour most of this week. Indeed I've been out for 16 days out of the last 23. Now I shall be staying at headquarters for about a fortnight. Touring at this season means that I get plenty of walking – about 7 miles on Saturday, and 10 or 11 yesterday.[88] The rivers are at their lowest now. We have had several stormy days lately, and today was a steady downpour. This has kept the weather pleasantly cool, but will make our work of Jute Restriction Propaganda[89] very difficult, as all the cultivators are taking advantage of this early rain to get their jute planted in double-quick time.

Madaripur, East Bengal
28 February 1937

Your letters of the 19th – on which you had written 'Please Forward' – arrived here this morning. I hope that my letter telling you of the breakdown of the Mysore plan arrived before you wrote your next letters. That breakdown is complete. I heard this morning from Thumboo Chetty that as the Govt. of Bengal had declined to lend my services, the Mysore Govt. would not make any further reference in the matter. He also said that they were very disappointed, and that Prince Jaya himself was looking forward to my coming, particularly for the Japan trip. The Mysore chapter may now be treated as closed.

I am glad that you had a chance of meeting Bill Empson.[90] Prima facie, I don't agree with his opinion that Margaret & Ronald should return to Singapore, if R. can get at all a reasonable job at home. . . .

There has been lots more rain this week, most unusual for the time of year. It's kept the thermometer down, and I'm still wearing grey flannel trousers. But I'm afraid I'll be donning my whites soon, and in a couple of months the heat will be excessive. The rain has brought on my flowers at last and I've got quite a good show of hollyhocks. The carnations are coming on too, but the sweet peas and nasturtiums are practically over.

There's not much to write to you about this week. Wednesday Thursday & Friday were hectically busy days of office work, & yesterday was almost as bad. I shall be in Madaripur all next week, as the 'Rosalind' is having her boiler cleaned. I have innumerable committees to attend next week, and life will be pretty full. There's one thing about this hard work – it doesn't give me time to worry about Mysore.

Indian politics are getting a bit lively, and if Congress decides not to accept office, things will be livelier still. Luckily in Bengal the Communal

Award has put the Mahommedans in power, & they are going to try to work the Constitution. The Moslem League (Conservatives) and the Proja Party (Labour) have formed a coalition under the leadership of Mr. Fazlul Huq, the Proja Party leader, & have issued a delightfully idealistic programme including the upsetting of the Permanent Settlement & the immediate introduction of free compulsory primary education. Where, one asks, will the money come from?

Notes

[54] Sir Michael Keane, K.C.S.I., C.I.E., joined the I.C.S. in 1898, and, after distinguished service in the United Provinces, became Governor of Assam in 1932. He died a few months after his retirement in 1937.

[55] Mrs. Blank was an extremely good pianist, and used often to be the soloist at the Calcutta Symphony Orchestra Concerts.

[56] I had met Walter Boulton and his wife Lorna on my previous visit to the Blanks in Shillong. They came to dinner my first evening there, and Lorna sang Elizabethan love songs to Walter's accompaniment. During the war, they did remarkable work for soldiers on leave from the Eastern Front in Calcutta, where he was Senior Chaplain of the Cathedral. Walter was Provost of Guildford from 1952 to 1961. (In the *cause célèbre* of the first Dean of Guildford – described in chapter 3, 'A Case of Patronage', of Paul Ferris's book *The Church of England* (1962) – my sympathies were almost entirely with the Boultons; and when I became the first Appointments Secretary to the Archbishops of Canterbury and York in 1966, the Guildford case – partly because of my long-standing knowledge of the principal *dramatis persona* – was engraved on my memory as an example of how patronage should *not* be exercised.)

[57] Rs. 700/- a month was equivalent to £630 a year. This in 1937 was a handsome salary for a young man of 25. There was really no time and little temptation to spend money in Madaripur: the wages of my five servants (including the gardener) would not have exceeded Rs. 80/- a month in all; food was very cheap; I had (and could have) no horse or car, and any travelling expenses on duty were refunded. One thing it *would* have been easy to spend money on was drink. . . .

[58] M. M. Stuart, C.I.E., O.B.E., entered the I.C.S. in Bengal in 1927.

[59] I was Returning Officer for the two Muslim constituencies of Madaripur East and Madaripur West. Separate electorates for Hindus and Muslims had been a feature of the 'Communal Award' made after the Round Table Conferences of 1930–32.

[60] The voting symbols were not as politically neutral as might have been supposed. There was keen jockeying by each candidate to have the plough as his symbol.

[61] Governor Landon was the unsuccessful (Republican) candidate for the U.S. Presidency in November 1936, when he was defeated by Roosevelt by 470 votes to 61.

[62] Water-hyacinth was 'a plant first brought quite innocently into Bengal as an object of beauty for a garden pond in Narayanganj [the jute port of Dacca] by George Morgan, then employed in the jute trade. From there it spread till every waterway in East Bengal began to be choked by it; navigation was obstructed. Every kind of measure to destroy it was tried but to no effect. It was not useful even as manure; though it contained phosphates, the quantity was so small as to make extraction unprofitable. (Sir Robert Reid, op. cit. p. 51). The 'demonstration', which could only be arranged in the cold weather, when the water-level was low, consisted of a mob of people, mostly schoolboys, immersing themselves in a stream and hurling the weed on to the bank –

where it was collected in piles to rot – to the accompaniment of the slogan 'Kochuripana dhongsho hok!' ('Destruction to the water-hyacinth!') Whether the exercise had any economic, in addition to propaganda, value is doubtful.

[63] The Petromax, though giving a brilliant light, also gave out much heat, which was unwelcome except in the cold weather. At some seasons of the year, it attracted hosts of flying insects of one kind or another, and so caused an entomological holocaust.

[64] The possession of a gun of any kind added greatly to the owner's prestige. Guns were of four categories – D.B.B.L., S.B.B.L., D.B.M.L., and S.B.M.L., which being interpreted meant double-barrelled breech-loader, single-barrelled breech-loader, double-barrelled muzzle-loader, and single-barrelled muzzle-loader. S.B.M.L.s were far the most numerous. Many weapons had pitted barrels and/or wobbly stocks, but unless the gun was potentially lethal (to the person firing it) the licence was generally renewed.

[65] The common ancestor was George Smith, M.P. (1765–1836). He had fifteen children, of whom one son was the Queen Mother's great-grandfather and one daughter was my great-grandmother.

[66] I cannot now imagine why I did not buy a wireless set, to lessen my isolation, as I could well have afforded one. Perhaps they were difficult to instal and maintain.

[67] Sir John Pilcher, G.C.M.G., Ambassador to Japan from 1967 to 1972, was at that time in the Consular Service in Tokyo, living in a flat in the Embassy. We were undergraduate friends.

[68] Previously the water-level had always been too high to allow walking.

[69] The wealthy candidate from Jalpaiguri was Golam Kibria, and I remember him only by name. The three local candidates I knew well – 'Badshah Mia', the Chairman of the District Board, already encountered in Letter of 2 August 1936; Abul Fazl, and Doliluddin Ahmed, both pleaders of the local Bar.

[70] 'Taxes' is too grandiloquent a word. The money was raised by extra rates levied by the riparian Union Boards – see Note. 27. The canal was five miles long, and was excavated at a cost of Rs. 3000/- (i.e. £400). the cost of excavation being just over Rs. 4/- per 'kua' (60 cubic yards). The excavated earth was used to construct a through road above flood-level for the whole length, some portions being new and others improvement of existing roads.

[71] Rai Bahadur Hira Lal Moulik, already mentioned in Letter of 27 September 1936.

[72] G. R. Mukerjee had come in the autumn to fill the vacancy caused by Niranjan Bardhan's departure. He was one of the very few Christian Magistrates in the Provincial Service, and was of much value in the communally tainted atmosphere of Madaripur.

[73] This watch is still going strong, forty years later.

[74] Michael J. Carritt had joined the I.C.S. in 1930, and had been Under Secretary in the Political and Appointment Department (renamed the Home Department in 1937) since the end of 1935. He was a popular and efficient member of the Service. His responsibility as Under Secretary included the handling of some political intelligence and all code and cipher telegrams. It caused consternation when it later transpired that, while Under Secretary, he had been an active and effective member of the Communist Party. He left the Service in 1939.

[75] I cannot now think that nothing was locally known, or at least suspected, about my possible move to Mysore, since the telegram quoted in Letter of 21 November 1976 had not been in code.

[76] The contestants for the Chairmanship were the sitting incumbent, 'Badshah Mia', and a much older and wiser lawyer of Faridpur, Maulvi Tamizuddin Khan, who later became a Minister.

[77] I had an office staff of about fifteen, excluding orderlies.

[78] The Treasury was in charge of a Sub-Deputy Magistrate, and I have only the haziest

recollection of my own responsibility – though I see from my diary entry for 31 March 1937, the last day of the old Constitution, that I had to spend four hours on a special verification of the entire contents of the Treasury. This included postage stamps as well as notes and coins. There were two 'shroffs' on the staff who were adept at counting notes and coins quickly. Most Treasury work was centralized at the district headquarters, and from time to time money was sent to and from Faridpur with an escort of armed police, if our supply of rupees became excessive or deficient.

79 The photograph did come out excellently – and I had great pleasure in showing it to the Hafizuddins' younger daughter and son-in-law, Mr. and Mrs. Shamsuddin, when they visited Cuddesdon in 1974.

80 The succesful candidate in East Madaripur was Maulvi Gyasuddin Ahmed – see Note 28. In West Madaripur, the exact result was Maulvi Abul Fazl 5,566 votes, Maulvi Golam Kibria 5,048 votes, and Maulvi Doliluddin Ahmed 1,175 votes. The fourth candidate, 'Badshah Mia', must have withdrawn – or been bought off. Only 24 per cent of the electorate voted.

81 The supervision of the Municipality was the District Magistrate's responsibility; but I evidently had a say in some of the membership.

82 The Brahmo Samaj was a purified form of Hinduism founded in 1830 in Calcutta by Raja Ram Mohan Roy.

83 Sir Bertrand Glancy, G.C.I.E., K.C.S.I., who was later Governor of the Punjab, from 1941 to 1946.

84 The Circle Officer, Madaripur, Maulvi Nurul Huq, was an older and less efficient officer than his opposite numbers in Palong and Sibchar. His handwriting was extremely difficult to decipher. But politically he kept his ear close to the ground, and this was valuable.

85 David Barclay Baron was a distant cousin and fellow-Wykehamist. He went into the Colonial Service and worked initially in Ceylon.

86 Normally the meat I ate was so-called mutton, but actually goat.

87 Robert Dutch has already been mentioned in Note 49, in the context of the 'Salt of Faridpur' Address of Welcome. He served in the I.C.S. from 1929 until Independence, and then went into Longman's, the publishers.

88 Both walks were in the neighbourhood of Palong, mainly in connection with the excavation of the canal referred to in my letter of 20 December 1936 and elsewhere.

89 Jute was the cultivators' main money-crop. If too much was planted, at the expense of paddy, the price went down; and with less paddy sown, the price of rice would later rise. The work of dissuading people from planting too much jute fell mainly on the Circle Officers.

90 William Empson, who had made his name with *Seven Types of Ambiguity* in 1930, occupied Chairs of English Literature in Japan and China, and was a friend of my sister and brother-in-law.

7 March 1937 - 27 June 1937

Madaripur, East Bengal
7 March 1937

This week has been a nightmare of incessant work. The weather is getting hotter. I could hardly bear to read your letters about the contemplated trip to Japan with the Prince. I shall not bore you with details of my work, but an SDO in these days is like a man trying to ride 10 horses at once – my ordinary judicial and office work is a whole-time job, quite apart from work in Schools, District Board, Co-operative Bank, and a thousand other institutions. I was never one to shirk work, but there are limits.

My garden, surprisingly enough, has quite a good display of flowers. Did I tell you about them last week? The hollyhocks especially are very fine. . . .

I really haven't got either the time or the spirits to write much this evening, but I'll add something if your letters come tomorrow morning.

8 March 1937

Your letters have come, but even now the news of the Mysore breakdown hasn't reached you.

Madaripur, East Bengal
15 March 1937

I have two sets of letters to answer this week, as you wrote the usual Friday letters and also extra ones on first receipt of the news about the Mysore disappointment. First let me thank you for ringing up Sir William at once. I most certainly welcome his writing to Col. Plowden and Glancy. That is one of my difficulties – that I can't put any pressure on my own behalf. Thumboo Chetty's last letter, however, struck such a note of finality that I'm not allowing myself to hope. But that letter was written as long ago as the 22nd February, and it is just possible that Sir William might revive the possibility.

I'm afraid you exaggerate the alleged compliment paid to me by the Bengal Govt. in wanting to retain my services. 'In the country of the blind the one-eyed man is king.'[91]

I was so glad to have news of Edward Woods's preferment as Bishop of Lichfield. One of the curses of Madaripur has been that my English correspondence has gone to the dogs simply for lack of time. I kept up with the Woods family regularly before . . .

I've had a very heavy week, partly at Madaripur & partly out on tour, but this evening I feel as if I was temporarily on top of my work instead of the work being on top of me. It is having to do 2 men's work that is really the difficulty here; I can tolerate the absence of company very well. If it were possible for me to get one hour off for exercise in the afternoon, and have some leisure for private reading and correspondence after dinner, I shouldn't mind working for the other 11 hours of the day. It will only be when I leave M'pur that I shall realize how hopelessly out of touch I have got with all my previous interests. My character will have changed a good deal too. When I came here I trusted & believed people unless I had definite proof that they were liars, and I believed in the value of friendliness. Now I never trust anybody, and I have learnt that the people here take advantage of friendliness....

I shall be going to Faridpur next week-end for the District Board Budget Meeting, which was postponed for a week. When there I shall hear the result of the Palong Abduction Case, which has been going on in the Sessions Court since the 1st. I fully anticipate a conviction, though I haven't the faintest doubt that the accused is innocent of this crime. His difficulty is that he spent all his resources in the trial before me, even up to briefing Mr. A. K. Fazlul Huq (who is going to be Bengal's first Chief Minister under the new Constitution). So he's not been able to get hold of good pleaders in the Sessions trial – probably he's not got even enough to bribe the jury with. The Hindus on the other hand got substantial help (Rs.500/-) from one of the Election Candidates, so the odds are heavily in their favour. Talk about British Justice! The son of the Chairman of the Municipality[32] here was recently sent to jail for 5 years in a political case (revolver-finding), and the Chairman tells me that his son was added to the other accused simply because of the personal animosity between himself and the Superintendent of Police. He may be lying (he often does) but it's certainly not beyond the bounds of possibility. Another big political case is brewing from Palong side; the secret police have unearthed a big hoard of proscribed literature.

The latest Old Wykehamist Register arrived this morning. Looking through it brought back many happy memories, and news of many friends. I am perpetually thankful for my 5 years at Winchester.

as from Madaripur, East Bengal
Palm Sunday, 21 March 1937

I'm writing once again from Faridpur, where I am as usual staying with the Hills for the District Board meeting. The Hills have now got another resident in the house, the new Additional Sessions Judge, called Dutch. He's been out about 5 years, and is still unmarried. I've not seen much of him....

The District Board meeting this month is the Budget meeting, which is a very long drawn out affair. We sat from 1.0 till 8.15 yesterday, with a short break at sunset, and will be sitting again today, probably again from 1.0 till

6.0. It was very like a bear-garden yesterday, as there was a surplus for the current year, and there was acrimonious discussion about the way it should be distributed. Madaripur emerged triumphant with Rs.8000/- for a most important road! Today we shall have a pretty stiff fight.

The verdict of the Binapani abduction case was given yesterday. As I expected, it resulted in conviction; the 3 Hindu jurors voted for conviction, and the 2 Mussalman jurors for acquittal. The jury system is absurd for communal cases. If the Sessions Judge had not been systematically working on behalf of the prosecution, he'd have had the decency to transfer the case to Dutch. The accused were clamouring for a European judge. I haven't heard the sentence yet. The case is sure to go to the High Court.

Madaripur, East Bengal
Easter Day, 28 March 1937

This letter will probably arrive at Waldershare the day before Margaret and Ronald, so I am addressing it to you all. I wish I could be with you, though I think the home-coming of both of us together would have been almost overwhelming . . .

I was fully intending to go to Barisal this week-end, but at the last moment I put my visit off. What I felt I really needed was a few days of comparative leisure here. I am sure I have chosen wisely;[93] the financial year closes on March 31st, and there are many last-minute things which need my personal attention. I am also being able to catch up a little of my personal correspondence. I may possibly go to Barisal in April, as there's a holiday on the 24th. Also, Father Fawssett is coming to Charmugria next week-end, so I shall get my Easter Communion after all. Above all I wanted the week-end to take stock of my position here, and decide whether to apply for a transfer or for leave.

I don't know what Sir Edward Blunt has written about the I.C.S.,[94] but it is very doubtful whether he will be able to represent the point of view of the younger men of the Service. It's one thing to sit in the Secretariat under an electric fan, with memories of work in the Districts when there were opportunities of both leisure and pleasure, and quite another thing to be doing the work I have to do.

It's very difficult for me to put my views coherently, for what I feel I need above all is to get away for a rest to restore my sense of values and my sense of perspective. But as there is this chance of a family council, I'll try.

First of all, there's the political conflict. My secret sympathies, anyway as far as Europe is concerned, are anti-Fascist, anti-Imperialist, & pacifist; all that has to be completely bottled down here. There's a big political case just been unearthed in the east of the subdivision. A gang of young men have been discovered with a complete Communist Library and a revolver to boot. The books are probably books with which Margaret and Ronald would be in complete sympathy, and you yourself Father have become a keen devotee of the Left Book Club. Of course I hold no sort of brief for the methods of these young men, and I hope they will all be sent to jail for good long terms. But this sort of work is very distasteful.

Then there is the moral conflict. The longer I stay here the lower does my standard of morality become. I live in an atmosphere of intrigue and underhand dealings, and it is a corroding atmosphere. . . .

Then comes the question of marriage. As long as I am in the junior ranks of the I.C.S., I shall not marry. It is absolutely unfair to ask any Englishwoman to live in a mofussil station in Bengal. The alternative is celibacy, in the monastic sense of never seeing a female face from week's end to week's end. A bachelor in England will at least have female relatives and friends, but my work is exclusively with men, so that practically speaking I live in a world populated by one sex. This is unnatural and abnormal.

A transfer might help things; I could at least start with a clean sheet and the experience gained in Madaripur. But I think a short spell of leave is indicated. I shall have 6 months due on full pay at the end of June. I shall probably put in for leave from June till October. In England I shall decide finally whether the I.C.S. game is worth the candle. If I decide that it is not, I shall look round for something more congenial; but I shall certainly not consider resignation of a post which is secure and well-paid, unless I have something to take its place.

Abdul Gafur and the other accused in the Binapani Abduction case have each been sentenced to five years imprisonment. So much for 'British justice'. The Sessions Judge's decision may be set right by the High Court, but Gafur is a ruined man, anyway.

One of the principal schemes I am undertaking for the betterment of the people is the excavation of a long canal from Bhojeswar to Bhedarganj. (I've probably mentioned this canal before).[95] Some mischief-makers in one village are trying to oppose this by filing a civil suit. The local 'munsiff' (Civil Judge) is in league with them, as he is of the firm but entirely mistaken idea that I have joined with the police to excavate the canal by force. My main work this cold weather has been the preparation of schemes of rural welfare (roads, wells, canals, village playgrounds) in the firm expectation of receiving a sum of Rs.20,000/-. Now Government has failed to sanction the amount, so all my promises will have to be broken.

What is the use of working in such conditions?

I am really sorry to send you a letter like this to greet the homecomers, but once the Easter holidays are over I shan't have time to write a long letter like this.[96]

Madaripur, East Bengal
11 April 1937

There's no development in the matter of getting a transfer from here, except that I got a surprise letter from Mrs. Larkin, who is now at Darjeeling, as Larkin[97] has had the luck to be posted as District Magistrate of Darjeeling. She said she was sure I must loathe Madaripur, and invited me to come and stay with them if I got too gloomy. I doubt if I shall be able to do that, but I hinted to her that if she would put in a word for me with the Powers That Be, a change of atmosphere would be very acceptable.

I've had some pretty strenuous touring this week, and the weather's unpleasantly hot. Touring in the launch is alright, but without it most uncomfortable. I had fixed the 7th for a big water-hyacinth Demonstration with the neighbouring subdivision,[98] but though a large number of people from Madaripur side penetrated to a remote part of the hinterland, the people of the other subdivision failed to put in an appearance at all! The place selected with a lowlying marsh, which is under water most of the year, and which is practically the birthplace of this foul weed.

Yesterday I didn't get back from tour till 11.30 p.m., as a meeting of school-teachers took about twice as long as I expected. 'Verba, non facta' is the local motto. Today, I am not feeling up to the mark, so I've not gone to office, as I want to be fit for 4 days' tour, mostly with Hill, from the 13th till the 17th.

The Congress impasse is most discouraging. All that the Indian people need is a gesture of good-will. Of course the Congress Ministers were asking an impossible thing of the Governors; now neither side wants to lose 'face' . . .

Madaripur, East Bengal
18 April 1937

I'm most annoyed at having caught another of my streaming colds, and a worse one than usual, practically like hay fever. However, today's the third day and I hope I'll be feeling brighter tomorrow. I'm experimenting with Sanatogen as a general tonic. The hot weather is bound to be a bit exhausting.

I was out on tour most of last week. I started off alone on the 13th, in the 'Rosalind', and did a useful day's work ending in a prize-giving at one of the innumerable High Schools in this subdivision. The next morning I was to have joined Hill & Hafizuddin, but the 'Rosalind' had anchored in a shallow river which she'd entered at high tide; while trying to get out we ran aground,[99] and got stuck for 4 hours till the tide came up again. It was very silly of the serang not to anticipate this difficulty.

The next two days I spent with Hill & Doha; it was a positive galaxy of officials. The occasion was the opening of a new Charitable Dispensary, which had been started by one of the wealthiest inhabitants of the subdivision, in memory of his deceased daughter. It was a great gathering of the clans of Palong Circle, and there were speeches innumerable; our host did us proud, and achieved the remarkable feat of providing ice-cream for lunch at the height of the hot weather in a place which is notoriously inaccessible, being 6 miles from the nearest steamer-station, and connected by no roads worthy of the name.

Friday was occupied by an inspection of a school by Hill and another public meeting for Rural Reconstruction. My cold had begun by then, so I was rather relieved when the Higher Officials cleared off. Their visits on the whole are an awful bore.

The Boyles leave for England tomorrow. I don't envy them the journey with 3 children plus a baby[100] in the hot weather. I shall miss them a lot. Their successors are called McReady, & I hear he's young & newly-married and (!) a member of the Oxford Group. I shall probably meet him tomorrow.

I can't think how my Easter Day letter got to you so soon, & I wasn't expecting an answer to it till next week. There are various points in it that I'd like to answer, but I'll wait till next week when my head is clear of this curséd rheum. . . .

Madaripur, East Bengal
25 April 1937

. . . Well, there's not a great deal of news this week. I've been at headquarters except for one quick & quite unnecessary excursion to the east of the subdivision, where the Collector was examining a big land dispute involving the neighbouring district. The temperature has fallen from the

100s to the 90s, as the two-month drought has broken at last. East Bengal never gets the excessive heat that one experiences up-country. My cold lingered on annoyingly, and even now I haven't thrown it off entirely. The taste of Sanatogen is rather unpleasant, but I suppose it's doing me good.

Did I ever tell you about the project of excavating a big canal, 6 miles long, on Palong side? I think I probably mentioned it, and also that we were restrained from excavating one portion owing to a disputatious individual who filed a civil suit. We have been trying for over a month to get the matter compromised, but he refuses to come to reasonable terms. All the rest of the work will be wasted unless some way can be found out next week, as the water is beginning to rise, and excavation will soon be impossible. This sort of thing is very discouraging.

Boyle's successor came to call this morning. I like the look of him; he's only about 29, I should say. He's fetching his wife from Calcutta in a few days...

P.S. My bearer returned at the beginning of the month. I was glad to get him back though he's a bit lazy.

P.P.S. I do indeed use my gramophone. It is a great solace.

Madaripur, East Bengal
3 May 1937

This letter will probably arrive on Coronation Day. You will, I expect, spend most of the day listening to the wireless. ... Are the Guilfords[101] using their old Coronation Robes? If so, it's a tribute to Lady G.'s figure. I'm afraid that my hope of hearing the Coronation Broadcast will not be fulfilled, as Stansbury is going off to the hills for a holiday, and anyway I shall be busy here. We have formed a Committee (as usual), and planned a programme including a police Parade, distribution of alms and rice to beggars, distribution of sweets to schoolchildren, prayers in the mosques and pujas in the temples, a procession, a football-match, and illumination of public buildings. We have budgeted for an expenditure of Rs.400/- (£30!), and it will be quite a job to raise the money. Fortunately, the thing is being managed mainly by non-officials.

I ought to be at office now by rights, but my long-standing cold, which I've never really shaken off, has gone to my throat and my voice has disappeared. So it's useless for me to attempt any judicial work. I'm taking a beastly gargle, and will be alright soon.

There's nothing else to comment on. Work has been heavy as usual, but

I'm not overworking myself as much as I used to. I read detective stories at mealtimes, which is a recreation. . . .

Father Fawssett is coming to Charmugria for Ascension Day, so I shall be able to make my first Communion since January 3rd.

Madaripur, East Bengal
10 May 1937

This is the first letter from a new pad of Air Mail stationery, so let it be a good one, even though my hand is sticking to the paper, and innumerable insects of various types are buzzing round, and going frequently into my hair and down my neck.

There is more news than usual this week. My cold & sore throat have gone at last. We've had a lot of rain and storms this week, with the result that for two or three days it was surprisingly cool, the minimum temperature going down to about 70° I suppose. Taking it all round, this has been a very kind hot weather so far; nothing excessive in the way of temperature. But then East Bengal is always cooler than West Bengal or North Bengal, by a few degrees. So what with one thing and another, I've cheered up a lot.

I've been at headquarters all the week, as the launch boiler needed cleaning. This was lucky as it enabled me to go over to Charmugria for Father Fawssett's visit. Originally he'd planned to come on the 3rd, so I planned to tour on 5th–7th. Finally he came on 5th & 6th, and as I said my tour programme being cancelled I was able to go over to Charmugria on both days. On the 5th we had an evening service about Coronation, and on the 6th (Ascension Day) we had a celebration. The two McReddies and an Anglo-Indian called Lucas were the other communicants. McReddie is not at all 'Groupy'; indeed I don't know if he is still a member of the Groups. . . .

On the 8th an exciting incident occurred to disturb the monotony of my daily work. I was in Court as usual at 2.15 p.m. when I was informed that there had been a riot at which the police had been obliged to use gunfire. These riots are quite common occurrences in the newly formed 'char' lands, where the titles to land have not yet been established, but firing by the police is an exceedingly rare occurrence, and always has to be followed immediately by a Magisterial inquiry into its justification. I hurried off to the place with Hafizuddin in the police launch; luckily it was less than an hour's journey from Madaripur about 6 miles up the river. After holding the enquiry, it appeared that the firing was fully justified. There were about

600–800 people on one side and 300–400 on the other, all armed with spears, or hatchets, or cudgels, or failing anything else with the usual missiles of clods of earth and potsherds. They were drawn up in two lines ready to attack each other. One Assistant Sub-Inspector[102] with a rifle and two unarmed constables happened to be in the locality by a very lucky chance. He tried to prevent them fighting, but they paid no heed at all, and after many warnings he fired 3 rounds, which missed completely (my opinion is that he missed deliberately, as he thought the crowd would disperse merely on the sound of gunfire). Then the larger party began attacking a homestead, so he fired again, 4 rounds in all, and two men fell, one on each side. This caused the crowd to disperse at last. He really handled the situation very effectively, though not strictly according to rule. Yesterday, when I was expecting to have a fairly free day, I was kept busy writing my report about the incident to Government.

In my next letter I'll tell you how Madaripur celebrated the Coronation. So far we've formed the inevitable Committee, & are collecting funds. We've drawn up a programme which includes a procession, distribution of alms & rice to beggars, & sweets to school children, a football match (in which I shall participate) and illumination of public buildings.

You said that I never mention the *New Statesman*. I read it most assiduously, and should greatly miss it if you didn't send it on. But its political views are very unhealthy for a young I.C.S. officer! In fact I used to censor it liberally before giving the Buxa Detenus their copy.

Madaripur, East Bengal
16 May 1937, Whit Sunday

Since I last wrote the Coronation has come and gone. It was celebrated with due éclat in various parts of the subdivision. Here, we started off with a meeting at which a 'message of loyalty' to Their Majesties was composed, read out and despatched to Government. Then a procession of all the schoolboys was organized, through the main street. It was rather a disorderly rabble headed by Hafizuddin and myself, and a discordant band-party. Next all the children dispersed to their respective schools, and were given sweets. Meanwhile, the distribution of rice and pice to beggars was going on. To our surprise, less than 500 beggars turned up, though we'd budgeted for 800. However, this will enable us to make both ends meet. We then closed down for the midday heat. In the afternoon, a football match was arranged, in which the officials beat the non-officials by 2 goals to 1. Bengalis are extremely good at football which they play with their bare feet. I found that I was deplorably out of training, but that was not surprising, as one can't go for a year without taking any strenuous physical exercise, and still remain in the same condition as before. I shall have to take to skipping or some such thing!

After this, I went over to Charmugria, and listened to the electrical reproduction of the Coronation Service on Corbett's wireless set. It came through excellently. I heard all the Service up to the Homage, and then I had to get back as it was nearly midnight. . . .

After the Coronation, I had two rather lazy days touring, mostly in connection with schools, in the north of the subdivision. It is impossible to do anything active in the middle of the day in the mofussil.

I have been reading and enjoying a very aged novel, namely, Sinclair Lewis' '*Main Street*'. It is a horrible picture of the vulgarity of the Middle West. I look forward to the receipt of '*Juan in China*', though I understand that it is not a patch on '*Juan in America*'. . . .

All the men of my year were asked whether they want to join the Foreign & Political, & I sent in the usual form. I don't think I've much chance of being chosen, as they're particularly keen on a knowledge of Urdu which of course one doesn't get in Bengal; also both Drucquer[103] and Kitchin are applying, and certainly not more than one will be taken from the same Province. However, I have been summoned to go to Simla from July 19–22, so I'm thinking of taking leave for the whole month & seeing a few places en route, though July, being just after the break of the monsoon, is not a good time for gadding about. Whether my application is successful or not, my trip to Simla may provide an excuse for shifting me from Madaripur. But by now, habit has practically made me resigned to Madaripur – 'Better the devil you do know than the devil you don't'.

Madaripur, East Bengal
24 May 1937

It's a very long time since I typed a letter to you, but as today is a holiday and I'm not writing against time, let me take the opportunity of refurbishing a rusty accomplishment. This machine of mine broke a key in January, and the Company sent a man to repair it, and in doing so he threw out the whole adjustment. As it happened, just at that time an official letter came saying that Government were about to renew their contract with Remington's for oiling and repairing office machines throughout the Province, and they would welcome any criticisms about past work. I dropped a delicate hint to the Company that if they didn't put my machine right pretty quickly, my reply would be unfavourable. They at once took my machine to Calcutta at their expense, and sent it back as good as new, all for nothing.[104] I felt quite justified in putting this pressure on the Company, as a hundred official letters are typed on this machine for every one personal one.

The holiday today is not, as you might suppose, for Empire Day, but for a Moslem festival called Fateha Duaz Dehan; but it is equally welcome, whatever the cause. All the same, I do seem to have had much more leisure this month than in March or April, though I have not been consciously slacking; the truth is that the whole tempo of Government slows down a little in the hot weather. This week has been marked by storms almost every day. They come mostly in the evening, but a particularly severe one on Monday afternoon revealed the inadequacy of the temporary office building; the windows and roof leak, and there is about an inch gap between the floor and the wall through which the rain drives in great quantities! During the rains last year these defects were hardly noticed, but the north-westers have found out the chinks in our armour. The P.W.D., or Public Works Department, is popularly known as the Public Waste Department, and it fully deserves its name.

I was out on tour on Friday and Saturday trying a Bad Livelihood case; there have been remarkably few of these lately, for which I am devoutly thankful, as they are a great addition to my work, and I hate the procedure. I had five in the first three months here, and only two since then. Next week-end I go to Faridpur for a District Board Meeting; it will be my first escape to civilization for two months. As Hafizuddin is not going, I'm not allowed to take the launch; mercifully the through steamer service started running last week, so the journey won't be quite so tedious.

The Air Mail and the ordinary mail both arrived this morning. First I must thank Mother for her truly brilliant effort in transcribing the Coronation Broadcast; it amplified the brief audience I had at the Corbetts' bungalow. Stansbury, by the way, is a nice old jute-wallah, who's been in Charmugria since the 90s! Father's letter was most interesting too, and I quite liked the Coronation stamp....

Your copy of Sir William's letter was distinctly encouraging, and I hope that his optimism will be justified. By today's post I also got a letter from Kitchin, from which I learn that Carritt thinks that I am quite likely to be taken into the F & P. Kitchin himself is not applying, as he thinks he has less chance than I; he hopes I will be taken, as that will leave the field more or less clear for him in the matter of the appointment of the Governor's Assistant Private Secretary,[105], which will soon fall vacant, and for which the odds are at present, according to him, slightly in my favour. It seems that whether my visit to Simla bears fruit or not – and after my disappointment about Mysore, I'm not banking on anything – I'm not likely to remain at Madaripur for very much longer. I have formally applied for leave from July 5th to 31st. My plans are vague at present, but I shall probably stay about a week in Calcutta, and then make my way to Simla by slow stages via Benares, Agra, and Delhi.

as from Madaripur, East Bengal
30 May 1937

I am writing this on board the river steamer 'Emu', which is one of the newest and most comfortable steamers belonging to the Company. We are sailing down the Ganges in the middle of a violent thunderstorm. The waves are quite formidable, and I am glad I am not making the journey in the 'Rosalind', for this reason, but only for this reason, as the steamer route is tediously circuitous.

There is really nothing to write about this week except my visit to Faridpur. It was preceded by four days of unusually hard work – quite like old times! For example, I was in office from 11.0 a.m. till 9.30 p.m. without a single break on Tuesday. But that was chiefly because there was an unusually large number of complaint petitions after an interval of two holidays.

I left for Faridpur on Thursday night, and it took me just 24 hours from door to door! The only event worth recording about the journey is that on board the steamer I fell in with a very nice young jute-wallah from Chandpur. The effect of a couple of pints of iced beer with him was to send me to sleep immediately after lunch; I dislike tepid beer, so I was comparatively 'out of practice'. My ordinary drink at Madaripur is lemon squash, lime juice, and cocoanut-water[106] – and lots of tea.

The Hills were the same as ever, except that the hot weather has thinned down Jeremy a little, to his considerable improvement but to his mother's great distress. Faridpur has been greatly improved by the introduction of electricity, which means not only the convenience of electric light, but the comfort of fans, and cold food & drinks from a refrigerator.

The District Board Meeting was a dull one, but as it was my first visit to Faridpur since March, I had many other files to talk over with Hill. Unfortunately he was so hectically busy with committees that I hardly had time to get in a word edgeways. I expect to find your latest letters awaiting me on my return, so I'll keep this open for the present. Nothing more to report about my contemplated visit to Simla.

Madaripur, East Bengal
9 June 1937

I have left my weekly budget rather late, but if I post this letter this afternoon, it should catch the mail in time. The reason for the delay is that I was out on tour over the week-end. Today being a holiday in honour of the King's Birthday, I am taking the opportunity to write. Incidentally, the King's birthday is really in December, isn't it? I suppose the idea is to split up the year into two halves for the purposes of the Honours Lists.

As usual there is nothing of overwhelming importance to write about Madaripur. Days at headquarters follow a pretty stereotyped routine, though some days there is a heavier post to be dealt with, other days there are more callers to be interviewed, and other days more criminal complaint-petitions are filed. But generally speaking, I have learnt to organize, postpone or neglect my work in such a way that I seldom get that harassed feeling which used to beset me in my first few months here.

On Sunday I spent a busy day at Palong. In the morning, I had to settle a dispute between two rival girls' schools! (This is quite in the day's work of an S.D.O.) In the afternoon, I initiated a scheme for keeping the Palong harbour clear of water-hyacinth during the rains, by storing it inside a bamboo stockade to rot. It will be an interesting experiment.

This afternoon I'm going over to Charmugria to hold an inquiry into the grievances of some ratepayers of the Municipality, and I shall stay on for a bit at the McReddies. I've been summoned to give evidence in a political case at Faridpur on the 16th, which completely upsets all my programme. I recorded a confession of one of the accused. This giving of evidence is a great nuisance. I'm shorthanded enough as it is, but when my 2nd and 3rd officers have to go off to Faridpur to depose, the work here gets very behindhand. It's all due to this wretchedly slow communication.

My plans for July have not advanced any further yet, except that I've written to a couple of I.C.S. men in Bihar and the United Provinces to see if there's any chance of meeting them.

Thank you for your letters of the 28th. . . . Margaret's *Basic English* contract sounds distinctly profitable. I hope she'll send me a copy when it's published. I wish *Basic English* could be boosted in Bengal. The amount of energy wasted by schoolboys cramming textbooks like *Ivanhoe* is something incredible.

Madaripur, East Bengal
20 June 1937

It is nearly 11.0 p.m., but if I don't write now I shall miss the mail as I'm going out on tour tomorrow. I have two letters from Mother to answer, and one from Father, enclosing two photographs which brought back most pleasant memories of the beauty of Waldershare in high summer. . . . There are one or two questions to be answered. . . . I can't say exactly when I'll sail in 1938, but probably about March. . . . I knew the son of the Governor of the U.P., Haig, at Winchester, who is following his father's footsteps in the I.C.S. in the U.P., so I wrote to him asking if we might meet on my way to Simla. Unfortunately he's in an out-of-the-way station far from Agra. But he very kindly offered to introduce me to the Collector of Agra, who might put me up for a few days, and I hope to be able to avail myself of the offer. . . .

The big event this week has been the visit of the Government Cinema Party, which gave three shows at the High School on Wednesday, Thursday & Friday. Propaganda films were shown about prevention of cholera, destruction of water-hyacinth, & care of children, and a long anti-terrorist film. The audiences were quite satisfactory, though the town people are more sophisticated than the villagers, who are sufficiently intrigued by the mere spectacle of 'moving pictures', whatever the subject-matter.

My confidential clerk, on whom I greatly rely, and of whom I am as fond as the master–servant relationship permits, is down with pleurisy.

The pressure of work this month has been unduly heavy, and I shall be thankful of the coming holiday.

Madaripur, East Bengal
27 June 1937

I can hardly believe that next week I am going on holiday. I have become so bound up in Madaripur that it will be quite strange to see a glimpse of civilization again, and to see unknown white faces. The last three months have passed very quickly. My plans are gradually becoming formulated. . . . I shall rejoin at Madaripur on the 1st August. Our correspondence is likely to become a bit disjointed next month. The letters you write on the 9th July may be addressed to *Cecil Hotel, Simla*, and those of the 16th and 23rd to the U.S. Club, Calcutta. I will write to you when and where I can; it is a pity that July is such a bad month for photography and sightseeing.

The monsoon has set in regularly now, and there is an alternation between heavy showers, drizzle, and cloudy windswept skies. The river is rising fast, but so far the erosion at Madaripur has been very little.

I have been on tour most of last week, and have just set off again. My trip on the 23rd & 24th was up to the north of Sibchar Circle, and was rather lazy on the whole, as far as actual work in the mofussil was concerned. But the tour gave me a much-needed opportunity to clear off some overdue judicial work.[107]

At long last, the dispute about the Bhojeswar-Bhedarganj khal has been compromised, and I can breathe freely. There is going to be an opening ceremony on the 1st July. I hoped Hill might be able to come to it, but he's otherwise engaged.

My second officer, Abdul Latif, has been ordered to take charge of the subdivision during my absence. Govt. hasn't deigned to send anybody extra, so the work will become appallingly behindhand, as both Latif and I are already doing a very full day's work each.

... I shall probably write my next letter from Calcutta – a pleasant thought.

Notes

[91] This remark was hardly complimentary to my fellow-civilians in Bengal. But we were very thin on the ground, so all had a certain scarcity value. As mentioned in Note 4, the total cadre of the I.C.S. in the Province was 185. At that time the population of Bengal was about 56 million.

[92] The Chairman of the Municipality was Babu Girindra Nath Rai Chaudhury. He had been a Rai Sahib, but, as one of the most prominent Congressmen in the area, had renounced his title. He and Rai Bahadur Hira Lal Moulik were the two leading members of the criminal Bar. Girin Babu, though a political opponent, was a likeable person and I had a considerable respect for his ability.

[93] In retrospect, my choice seems very unwise. It would have been much better in every way to have spent Easter at Barisal. I did not eventually visit it until 1945.

[94] *The Indian Civil Service* by Sir Edward Blunt had just been published by Faber. The dedication was 'To MY WIFE who has spent thirty-four years with me in India, and knows as much about the I.C.S. as I do'. My apprehension that he might not be able to represent the point of view of the *younger* members of the Service was not unreasonable. But at the time it was a valuable publication, which filled a gap.

[95] See Letter of 20 December 1936.

[96] From my diary it is clear that I did write home on 4th April. Looking at the entries for the preceding days – which incidentally included the inauguration, on 1st April, of Provincial Self-Government – I can only suppose that it was such a gloomy missive that my parents did not keep it. My diary entry for March 31st ended: 'Was woken at midnight to take dying deposition of a man whose penis had been cut off. He was quite incoherent. Rather a symbolic way of seeing the new Constitution in!'

[97] A. S. Larkin, C.I.E., joined the I.C.S. in Bengal in 1921 after war service. He had been District Magistrate of Rajshahi from 1933 to 1936, and had been posted to Darjeeling in March 1937 after a spell of leave.

[98] The neighbouring subdivision to the west was Gopalganj, the S.D.O. of which was

a Deputy Magistrate, Babu Kanai Lal Banerjee. Life in his subdivision was even more amphibious than in mine.

[99] One of my most vivid aural memories from Madaripur is the sing-song voice of the serang's son standing in the bows of the *Rosalind*, casting the line and lead, and announcing the depth – 'Sharay doo bahm – doo bahm ek hart – doo bahm milay nai' (two-and-a-half fathoms – two fathoms one cubit – not quite two fathoms).

[100] It is strange that I have absolutely no recollection of even the existence of the Boyle children. Though it was nearly always in the evening that I met the parents (when the children would have been in bed), I would have expected to remember something, at least of the arrival of the baby.

[101] The Earl and Countess of Guilford lived at Waldershare Park; he was the patron of my father's living.

[102] The ranks of the subordinate police under Hafizuddin were: Inspectors (two) supervising a group of four or five police stations; Sub-Inspectors, in charge of police stations; Assistant Sub-Inspectors; Head Constables; and Constables. A typical police station, with a population of 100,000 or so, would be manned by one sub-inspector, a couple of 'A.S.I.s', and about ten constables, with an armoury of a dozen rifles. It simply was not true that the British Raj governed by force of arms.

[103] Seth Drucquer and I had led curiously parallel lives. He was a contemporary of mine at Winchester, but a scholar; he went up to Cambridge a year before me, to Trinity Hall; he passed into the I.C.S. the same year, and was sent to the same Province. He was killed in an air crash between Calcutta and Delhi in August 1944.

[104] I used this machine until 1965, and it is still in working order. It never again had such hard labour as at the hands of my Confidential Clerk. It seems odd that no official machine was provided.

[105] There were only three posts in Calcutta available for junior Civilians: Assistant Private Secretary to the Governor, Under Secretary Home Department, and Under Secretary Finance Department.

[106] The liquid from the inside of an unripe cocoanut, called 'dahb', was a most refreshing cold drink, obtainable whenever and wherever I was on tour, and as safe to drink as unboiled water was dangerous.

[107] This work included, characteristically, one 'bad livelihood' case (in which I convicted all five accused), and two 'section 144' injunctions.

5 July 1937 - 7 November 1937

Bengal United Service Club, Calcutta
5 July 1937

I've just arrived in Calcutta, & will scribble off a few lines to catch the mail which leaves tonight.

I was pretty busy clearing things up at Madaripur last week. The opening of the Canal on the 1st went off very well indeed as we were lucky to get an absolutely perfect day for it. Rain would have spoilt everything. I handed over charge to my 2nd officer yesterday and left Madaripur without a pang.

I've just written to Mr. Weller of the Cambridge Mission to Delhi suggesting that I might stay there from the 14th till the 17th.

There's nothing of interest to say now, except that I'm feeling distinctly light-hearted at getting away from my benighted bog. I'll write a long letter next week.

at Clark's Hotel, Benares
10 July 1937

I sent a hurried scrawl to you just after I'd reached Calcutta, and promised to make my next letter a better one. I spent Monday afternoon in shopping and getting a most welcome haircut. This is a thing I always look forward to when I come to Calcutta, for my deft little Japanese barber is a great contrast to the untrained and hesitant Madaripur fellow. I spent the evening with Douglas Henderson, seeing *Captains Courageous* as a film, and dining with him at the Saturday Club,[108] which, since his wife's departure for England, is practically a second home to him.

The next morning I went to the dentist soon after breakfast; to my great satisfaction, only one hole was discovered, which was pretty good after more than a year. Then I went to the Secretariat, and saw various officials about personal and Madaripur concerns. I lunched with Douglas H. In the afternoon, I had a practice game of squash, which I greatly enjoyed; I last played at Buxa, so I was out of training and out of practice. I spent the evening again with Douglas, he treating me to dinner & I treating him to a mediocre film. He is really a most hospitable person, and I think he enjoys seeing somebody not of the usual Calcutta crowd.

This brings us to Wednesday. I forgot to tell you that on my arrival in Calcutta, whom should I see but Mr. Blank, who had come up from Shillong for some conferences. Mrs. B. has just returned to England, & expects to be there for the next 2 *years*. Poor B.![109] On Wednesday, he took me out as an extra guest to the Sandrés. Prof. Sandré is head of the Calcutta School of Music, organizes and conducts the Symphony Concerts, and is generally responsible for any good music that is heard in Calcutta; so I was glad of an introduction. He has a Scots wife. I had a most pleasant evening with Maurice Curtis and Hirtzel,[110] whose names you may remember from one of my former visits to Calcutta. They stood me dinner and a film, and I was most interested to find that Curtis' brother,[111] who is an I.C.S. man in the Political, is at present posted at Simla, so I shall certainly call on him; he may prove a friend in need.

On Thurday I didn't do very much except see over the Bose Institute in the morning, and have another game of squash in the afternoon. I'd recently been reading a life of Sir Jagadish Bose, who is the greatest scientist India has produced, and, next to Rabindranath Tagore, is the most famous living Bengali; so I was interested to see the place where all his disciples are following out the lines of research suggested by his highly original work in plant-physiology. That evening, I caught the Punjab Mail. As I'm not getting Travel Allowance for this trip, I'd decided to travel 2nd,[112] which saves at least Rs.100/-. I found that a berth had been reserved for me in a carriage stuffed with other people, so I changed to a non-reserved berth and had the carriage to myself the whole way to Benares.

I reached here yesterday morning and went to the only decent hotel in the town. I spent the morning sight-seeing, being taken round by a definitely intelligent guide attached to the hotel. We did the usual trip up the river, looking at the Maharajas' palaces which line the river-front, the sacred bathing-ghats, and the burning ghat. It is somewhat incongruous in the heart of Hinduism that from the river much the most prominent building is a mosque with tall minarets. Then we looked at some of the temples, which were not awfully exciting, and of course with the usual filthy crowd of beggars. In fact Benares itself is distinctly disappointing for anybody to whom India is not absolutely new. The iconoclast Aurungzeb saw to it that all the really old & interesting temples were wrecked.

Today I saw the far more interesting Buddhist remains at Sarnath, about 5 miles out from Benares. Buddha is said to have preached his first sermon there, so it is a great centre of pilgrimage for Buddhists. There are a number of buildings and sculptures dating back to the time of Asoka, 250 B.C. Luckily it was a very fine morning, so I was able to take some photographs. I shall later send you prints of any successful ones.

I suppose this letter conveys the impression that I have had a pretty full week, but actually I've had a lot of spare time. I'm purposely not filling every minute of the day, as it's pleasant to be lazy. I'm eating and sleeping more than usual; in fact I've spent most afternoons having a siesta and/or reading one of Dorothy Sayers' excellent detective stories.

Your last letters didn't give much news. . . . My next letter will be from Simla. I'm not keeping a Journal for this trip, as it's not a solely sightseeing trip, and I keep my own diary anyway.

Cambridge Mission, Delhi
15 July 6937

I leave Delhi tonight, and the Air Mail leaves tomorrow morning, so I shall take the opportunity of sending home a letter in record time. I last wrote from Benares; since then I have had a very happy week.

I spent most of last Sunday in the train, travelling to Agra in a rather crowded carriage; I was met there by Mr. Evans, the Collector, whom I liked on first sight. It was too late that evening to do anything but take a brief drive to the Taj, which I saw under bad conditions, as the sky was overclouded. But I returned next morning, and had a thorough visit in brilliant sunshine. For me to praise the Taj is to gild the lily; I will only say that its beauty is greatly enhanced by its setting in the gardens; until Lord Curzon's time they were overgrown with jungle, and the building cannot have been nearly so impressive then. In the afternoon, I went over Agra Fort, where there is a tremendous lot to see; the Pearl Mosque is particularly lovely. The weather was still fine; indeed it has been fine all the time till this afternoon. Evans was greatly lamenting the shortage of rain, & the fields certainly looked very dry.

The next day (Tuesday), I went to see Akbar's tomb before breakfast. This was also most impressive; Akbar means great, and he certainly deserved his name. Then I hired a taxi, and drove out to Akbar's deserted city of Fatehpur Sikri, where I spent a couple of most interesting hours clambering about the ruins. (Actually most of the buildings are in a very good state of preservation.) The whole city is built in red sandstone. It was used for only 16 years, and then the capital was shifted to Delhi.

I left Agra after tea, by the Mail Train, which takes only 4 hours to Delhi. Evans was an exceedingly pleasant host, and it was far more interesting than staying in a hotel. I was met here by Christopher Robinson,[113] whom I like very much. He's a son of Canon Robinson of Winchester (Canon from 1908 till 1932, I think) so we found a great link. The only other members of the Brotherhood at present in residence are Weller and Stokes. Weller is an older man. Do you know any of the three? It is really most refreshing to breathe a Christian atmosphere for a change.

Yesterday morning, Weller took me for a long tour of exploration of New Delhi; we went on bikes, which was a very hot method of progression, but meant that one saw more. It is planned on a most lavish scale. The Secretariat buildings are successful,[114] but I didn't much like the Dome on the Viceroy's House. The Church of the Redemption is satisfying inside, but fussy and undignified outside.

In the afternoon, I explored the Delhi Fort, which is finer than the one at

Agra. Then Christopher Robinson took me out in his car to see some of the earlier cities (there were seven Delhis in succession).

This morning I saw some of the Mission Work (the Boys' School & St. Stephen's Community), and also St. Stephen's and St. James' Churches, which both have considerable historic interest. I am soon going out for another trip to the earlier cities, and then I shall have to leave. My visit here has been all too short, as there is a tremendous lot to see in Delhi.

. . .Whatever happens to my application at Simla, this trip will have been well worth while, not only for the holiday, but also for the impression I have got of India outside Bengal. So far I haven't spent long enough in any one place to get my photographs developed. I have taken a large number of interesting ones under good conditions, and I am very much hoping they will be successful.

at Cecil Hotel, Simla
22 July 1937

There's a good deal to write about this week. I enclose a number of my more successful photographs.[115] They are all marked, so I needn't say anything more about them, except to add that I've had quite good enlargements made of the four prints marked E.

I found two lots of letters awaiting me here, and I will answer these before going on to my own news. . . .

I wrote last just before leaving Delhi. I stopped for a day at a place called Solon, halfway up the hills, in order to see a Trinity friend, Henry Winnington-Ingram (a nephew of the Bishop) who is a Lieutenant in the Worcestershire Regiment, and has been stationed at Solon for the hot weather. He was due to return to Sialkot in the Punjab on the 17th, so it was a very lucky coincidence that we just managed to see each other. He is the first of my England friends that I've met since 1934.

On my arrival here, I found the familiar face of Seth Drucquer (whose name you must surely know by now) to greet me. He is also trying very hard to get into the Political, and will be more disappointed than I if he is not chosen; personally I shouldn't think he had much chance, as his politics are very Left Wing, and he's not made a good impression in Bengal. He has the room next door to mine, and we feed at the same table. It has certainly been more pleasant to have a companion here this week.

The hotel is a very comfortable one,[116] and I've got a nice room, where I've been spending a good deal of time reading, & writing many overdue letters to English friends. This may seem rather an unenterprising way of spending my time, but actually there's precious little to do, at this time of the year, when it's usually misty or raining, unless one knows a great many people here, which of course I don't. We restricted our calling simply to the people in the Foreign and Political Department, and to the civilians from Bengal. However, in case you should get the wrong impression that I've been wasting my time here, I'll give you a catalogue of my activities.

On Sunday, I went to the early service, which was well-attended, and very nicely taken. Both in the morning, and after tea, Seth & I paid calls. Distances in Simla are enormous, but one looks so decadent taking a rickshaw that I don't unless I'm going to a really far place. I've had plenty of exercise this week. Simla is not nearly so cold as Darjeeling, nor is the scenery so grand. But it is of course extremely pleasant to be out of the plains. On Sunday evening I again attended church and it was quite fun to be able to exercise my lungs again.

Monday was the great day, fixed for my interviews at the Foreign and Political Secretariat. I went with two other men, Knight of my own year from the United Provinces (whom I was very pleased to meet again), and Pringle of Bengal, a year senior to me. Pringle is Asst. Private Secretary to the Governor of Bengal, and for that reason may have a bit of a pull over us. I gather that they are very likely to take one man from Bengal, and quite certain not to take more than one. In addition to the people already mentioned, there are 2 people from the Punjab and 1 from Bombay. There are likely to be about 3 vacancies, one in October and two in March.

The various Secretaries of the F & P played battledore-and-shuttlecock with Pringle, Knight & myself, and by 3.0 I'd seen all six interviewers. They were Col. Parsons, the Foreign Secretary, Mr. Corfield, the Political Secretary, Mr. Lothian, the Federation Secretary, Col. Gaisford, the Deputy Political Secy., Major Hay, the Deputy Foreign Secy., and Mr. Egerton, the Deputy Federation Secy. They were all very pleasant and friendly, and chatted for about 10 minutes each, chiefly about my work in Bengal, and Sir William Barton, and Winchester & Cambridge. Of course everybody here knows that Bengal is a place to be escaped from, so there was no point in disguising the fact that this was *one* of my motives for appearing. On the whole, I was not conscious of 'dropping any bricks'.

The main event of the next day was the Viceregal Lunch. I enclose a newspaper cutting from which you will see that Pringle & Knight were again my companions. The lunch itself was not awfully exciting, though everything went smoothly thanks to the efficient ADCs. Pringle & Knight were next to the Viceroy,[117] so they had the difficult job of making lunch-time conversation, and at the same time revealing their suitability for appointment to the F & P. I luckily was able to keep the two functions separate, as H.E. gave me 5 minutes interview after lunch. He asked me details about my work in Bengal, which I was fortunately able to answer. He was quite easy to talk to. I learn that his impression counts more than all the six Secretaries put together. By the way, the two permanent Secretaries, Sir Bertrand Glancy & Sir Aubrey Metcalfe, are both on leave in England; this probably made the interviews easier, as they would have been less affable than the officiating men.

On Tuesday night I dined with Mr. & Mrs. Curtis. He was in the Punjab I.C.S., and is now in the Political Department, at present working as Asst. Commissioner of the Punjab Hill States. I know his brother Maurice quite well; he is in one of the Calcutta firms. I liked the Curtises; Mrs. C. was particularly pleasant, quite unspoilt by Anglo-India, and rather reminding me of Mrs. Miller.

Yesterday I dined with Col. Gaisford and John Shattock,[118] whom I knew in Bengal, as Asst. Private Secretary to the Governor (Pringle's predecessor). I was glad to see Shattock again, though he looked very tired and overworked. He confided to me that I'd made a good impression on the Secretaries, but my Mysore experience has taught me not to build too much on that.

However, this has made me think about the question of leave, and I may as well put the whole position about this, as far as I can estimate it. The appointments to the F & P will not be made till October anyway. I will then be informed either (1) that I am appointed to a job straight away, and directed to join at once. In this case I should almost certainly have to postpone my leave. I should try to get leave in October 1938, and take it for a whole year. (2) I may be appointed to a job which will not fall vacant till March or April. In this case, I should apply to the Bengal Govt. for granting me immediate leave for 4 or 5 months. In the off-season it would be easy to book a passage at a day's notice. Of course it would be a bit dismal taking leave in the winter, but I should be able to see you, and see my friends. Also, if Margaret & Ronald have to return to Singapore, I should get the chance of seeing them too. (3) I may be told that they are retaining my name for consideration in next year's appointments. (4) I may not be wanted at all. In both these contingencies, I should return to Madaripur till March '38, and then take leave as previously arranged from March till October. I will not venture to prophesy what will happen, beyond saying that I think contingencies (2) & (3) are more likely than (1) & (4). You don't need me to tell you that I am longing to see you and England again, but a chance of getting out of Bengal must *not* be neglected, even though 'hope deferred maketh the heart sick'.

Have you read Emily Eden's *Up the Country*? The Curtises lent it to me, and it is perfectly fascinating, and particularly appropriate, as it describes her journey from Calcutta to Simla just a hundred years ago. I'm sure Mother would enjoy it enormously.

Bengal United Service Club, Calcutta
29 July 1937

I shall have to be very quick about writing this letter as the Air Mail goes from the Club in half an hour. I found letters from you all awaiting me on my arrival here on the 27th, and another letter came yesterday. . . .

I left Simla on Friday afternoon, and had a long, hot & dusty journey to Asansol which I reached early on Sunday morning. Chambers you may recall as one of my friends at Settlement Camp.[119] He married last February, and this was my first meeting with his wife. She, like he, is Yorkshire – very pleasant and friendly, and intelligent and pretty into the bargain. So he's done well for himself. They both seemed very happy. A greater contrast between Asansol and Madaripur can hardly be imagined. Asansol is in the extreme west of Bengal, predominantly Hindu, with a scarcity of water, and a large European population owing to the mining and steel industries. It is one of the most coveted subdivisions, but is, by a very proper convention, practically reserved for young married S.D.O.s. I stayed there two days and laughed more during those two days than I have in the last 12 months!

Since coming to Calcutta, I've been pretty busy with shopping and one thing and another. I've just bought a gun – at long last – from Manton's, not a second-hand one, as their selection was a poor one, but a not-too-expensive new one of their own make. I don't see much prospect of using it, anyway till the cold weather.

Yesterday I dined with the Hoggs,[120] and explained the prospects of the F & P to Hogg; so if, as I suggested in the last letter, I have to put in for winter leave at short notice, there should be no difficulty. This afternoon, I attended the historic occasion of the opening of the Legislature under the new Constitution. Sir John Anderson made a good & eminently constitutional speech. The Congress Members of the Legislature very rudely absented themselves.

This evening I'm having Maurice Curtis to dinner at the Club. You will remember that I saw his brother Gerald at Simla.

I leave for Madaripur tomorrow, & feel as fit as a fiddle. This holiday's been infinitely worth while.

Madaripur, East Bengal
7 August 1937

Well, here I am writing from the familiar old address, though actually I'm at the moment making my way to Faridpur in the 'Rosalind' with Hafizuddin, for the District Board meeting.

I got back on Saturday morning, and spent most of the day unpacking, tidying up my bungalow – which I found in apple-pie order – and talking to Hafizuddin and Abdul Latif, in order to pick up the threads of the administration after my month's absence. I took over charge formally the next day, & occupied myself with reading the important files and letters that had been received and sent in July. So on Monday I felt in a position to take up my ordinary routine work without feeling that I'd lost touch. Latif has done very well in carrying on, and there's much less congestion of the criminal work than I anticipated.

I got rather a shock on the 4th when I got a telegram saying that the Commissioner was coming to Madaripur on the 5th, which didn't give me much time to prepare. The present Commissioner is Hector Wilkinson, a friend of Charles and Rhoda Miller, and an exceptionally nice man.[121] Everything went off very smoothly on the 5th, even though he arrived 1½ hours before he was expected. We walked to see Sakuni, which is probably to be the new Subdivisional headquarters; I think I succeeded in convincing Wilkinson of the need of a good motorable road connecting Sakuni with Madaripur and Charmugria. (Actually, the river has not been cutting at all yet this year, so the Sakuni scheme may possibly be abandoned.) In the afternoon, we went to Palong and Bhojeswar, and he saw some of the Bhojeswar Canal, and was quite pleased with our work.

Inspecting Officers never come singly, and the District Judge, whom I strongly dislike, is at Madaripur this week-end. However, he will be principally occupied with the Civil Courts. I shall be hurrying back to Madaripur tomorrow, partly on his account.

People seem pleased to see me back again, as there were rumours that I was not going to return; and everybody says that I look much better for my holiday. And I certainly feel that I have recovered a zest for life, which I had rather lost before.

. . . I read Kipling's '*Something of Myself*' on my way back here. It was interesting, but told one too little about the latter part of his life. At present I'm in the middle of Liddell Hart's *The Outline of the War*.

Madaripur, East Bengal
14 August 1937

I am doing an almost unprecedented thing – writing this letter in my study at 9.0 a.m. on a weekday, a time when I am almost invariably engaged with correspondence and/or callers. But the rain has kept the callers away today, I cleared off all the pending files last night, I have dealt with today's post, and, though my confidential clerk[122] is ticking merrily away on my Remington, I have no immediate work on hand till office-time.

I wrote last week just before I arrived at Faridpur. My visit there was very unsatisfactory this month. All the files that I was anxious to get through quickly had been delayed by Hill or by his office, who rival each other for slowness. The one item of the District Board agenda which interested me was postponed, but even so the habitually loquacious members managed to talk a lot of bosh for 3 hours and more. Then, just when I wanted to watch an important football-match in which a school team from Madaripur was taking part, I had to attend a tea-party at the Hills. . . . In the evening one of the Faridpur zemindars, who is a member of the Legislative Assembly and the most influential man in the District Board, gave a huge dinner-party, to which all the leading officials and non-officials of the town were invited. The dinner was good, but afterwards the officials insisted on playing bridge, which I thought was very rude; I reluctantly had to make up a four.

On my return, I was kept busy escorting the District Judge round from place to place in Madaripur. He really is a nasty piece of work, horribly conceited,[123] and far too friendly with the pleaders & mukhtears, trusting their words against the magistrates. He brought no less than 35 relatives and hangers-on in the launch, packed in like sardines! His judgements are very erratic, and it will be a great relief to the District when he retires, which will mercifully be pretty soon.

I went out on tour for a couple of days on Sibchar side. One morning I intended to spend in a water-hyacinth demonstration; on arrival there were neither people nor water-hyacinth – a lamentably bad 'bandabast' by the Circle Officer.[124] Apart from that, there is little to note except much rain, and the steady rising of the river. I am reading Sir Francis Younghusband's *Everest: The Challenge*, and have just finished one of Miss Compton-Burnett's earlier novels *Brothers and Sisters*.

I am probably soon having a change in my staff. My bearer revealed to me that my old cook is a habitual smoker of 'ganja'[125] (a drug rather like opium), so I shall probably sack him. In the meantime, my bearer is going to take a little leave, to see his wife who is ill. While he is away, I shall try a substitute who knows both bearer's and cook's work. If he's satisfactory, I shall keep him on when Hedayet returns, and get rid of my old rogue of a cook, who can't act as a substitute bearer. This will be an advantage when I'm on tour, as Hedayet doesn't know much about cooking.

as from Madaripur, East Bengal
21 August 1937

I am actually writing this after dinner on board the 'Rosalind' in an isolated 'char' land to the extreme east of the subdivision. I am in the middle of a 5 days' tour in Palong Circle, from which I shall return on Tuesday. I am taking my new cook-bearer with me, and I have already decided that he is heaps better than my present man as a cook; actually he is practically as good as Hedayet in bearer's work – I've let Hedayet get a bit slack. He's gone off to see his family, and will return on the 5th September.

August is a great month for inspecting officers to come to Madaripur, because it becomes so much more accessible in the Rains. I have already had the Commissioner, the District Judge, and the Director of Public Instruction, and I expect the Collector, the Inspector-General of Police, and the Inspector-General of Registration before the month is out. However, no Minister has come my way yet, for which I am duly thankful. The Director of Public Instruction, who is, in the sphere of education, inferior only to the Education Minister & Secretary, is a very pleasant man called Bottomley,[126] whom I had met in Rajshahi. He came to M'pur on the 18th, and visited the Girls' School and Charmugria H.E. School, where he promised grants for rebuilding expenses and a playground respectively – a very encouraging visit! He also dined with me, and it was a pleasure not to talk shop.

The I.G. of Police is the head of all the police in Bengal, so he's a very big noise indeed. He is bestowing a great honour in visiting a little place like Palong. There will be the usual sort of reception with songs & garlanding, and lots of insincere speeches of adulation. Nine people out of ten in Palong hate and fear the police, but dare not say so.

as from Madaripur, East Bengal
29 August 1937

Your last letters of the 13th arrived just an hour after I posted my last missive, but this week a magnificent long letter from Mother has just come, & I shall be able to answer it by return of post. You may notice the postmark is Gopalganj, which is the headquarters of the south-western subdivision of the district, and the scene of the annual District Union Board Conference today. (You may remember that it was held at Madaripur this time last year.)[127] There will be a positive flotilla of launches there, as the Commissioner, Wilkinson, is coming from Dacca to open the Conference, and Hill is occupying another launch with his family, and Doha a third, while Hafizuddin & I bring up the rear. I shall try to take a photograph of the fleet!

This week has been a pretty hectic one – quite like old times! I got back from my long tour on Monday, so was kept pretty busy with an accumulation of work on Tuesday, and I didn't get dinner till 10.0 owing to a protracted girls' school committee meeting. On Wednesday afternoon, the Inspector-General of Police, by name Farmer,[128] arrived. He's the head of all the police in the Province, & is therefore a man of great importance; he's done about 30 years' service; his appearance resembles his name. We had a terrific reception for him at Palong on the 26th. Mercifully it didn't rain. There were literally thousands of people, though whether they came voluntarily or under police pressure I am unable to say. It struck me that there was a good deal of eyewash; however, I remained discreetly in the background, & let the police run their own show.

The next day, Friday, Hill was due to arrive in the afternoon, & I'd carefully arranged a programme for him at Charmugria, which he'd never visited before. A visit to the school & a big tea-party had been arranged, but he didn't turn up till 6.0, and all the arrangements were thrown out. The European members of the Charmugria community were justly annoyed, and I have seldom felt so embarrassed.

To make things more difficult, Hill told me that the Commissioner would be arriving the next morning (Saturday) and would be glad to interview the leading officials and non-officials of the town. A Commissioner's visit at a day's notice is no joke, & I had to get up at 5.0 to make the necessary preparations. However, all went off well, and I gave quite a successful dinner-party last night, & played vingt-et-un till midnight. So I'm feeling a trifle yeary today. However, this trip to Gopalganj will be a rest-cure.

Madaripur, East Bengal
4 September 1937

You have been wonderfully good in writing to me so often during your holiday, and I am throwing my work aside to catch the outgoing mail tonight. . . .

I believe you once said that Ld. Guilford knew Lord Brabourne.[129] Is Lord B. coming home before taking over Bengal? I heard so, but he was due to relieve Sir John Anderson in November, and Sir Roger Lumley has only just sailed for Bombay. I ought to know the plans of Bengal's future Governor, but I stupidly don't. If he does come home, Ld. G. might slip in a word for me, as between you & me I've got quite a good chance of getting Pringle's job as Asst. Private Secretary to the Governor, if I don't get the Political, & it might just tip the balance if Ld. Brabourne had heard my name before.

The trip to Gopalganj was quite a holiday, & was rounded off by dinner on Hill's launch, with just the Commbissioner & myself as guests – an I.C.S. dinner with the Police left in the outer darkness! The Hills are coming here next week again, he to inspect my office. This week has been uneventful, but fully occupied with lots of hard work. I'm going to be out on tour for most of the rest of the month, as I've planned an exceptionally heavy tour programme. I enclose a spare programme, which may interest you. I've added some explanatory notes.

Madaripur, East Bengal
11 September 1937

The past week has been quite interesting. I was kept busy most of Sunday with two School Committee meetings, & other work in my bungalow. I spent Monday in the mofussil, leaving early in the morning & returning at dusk to find that the Hills had reached Madaripur a few minutes before me.

The river had chosen this awkward moment to stage an exceptionally rapid rise, and almost before I knew where I was, the whole compound and 'drive' were under water just like last year in August. So I again had to get a landing-stage constructed leading to my western verandah, to enable my guests to come to dinner on the evening of the 7th. I had the Hills, the McReddies, Hafizuddin & Corbett to dinner, so we were quite a party. We played vingt-et-un afterwards till midnight. The next day was spent by Hill in inspecting the criminal records. He did this with his usual thoroughness, so much so that he didn't get through the work nearly as soon as he intended, & was therefore unable to inspect some other departments – for which I was devoutly thankful, as they were not up to the mark! It was rather difficult moving about these days, with the water-level so high, and I made full use of my Wellington boots.

On the 9th morning, I had arranged a big water-hyacinth clearance demonstration, which was a great success. The three High schools played up very well, and there must have been nearly 300 boys helping. We cleared a whole tank, & part of a stream which had long been an eyesore. Hill was quite pleased.

On the 9th afternoon, Hafizuddin, Latif & I left together in the 'Rosalind' for Faridpur, & the Hills went on a little later to Gopalganj. We halted for the night en route, & reached Faridpur by midday yesterday. I had gone in order to depose in a big political case. My deposition was not nearly such an ordeal as I expected, & only took an hour. I stayed with Sarkar, the Additional S.P. The visit was interesting because it gave me an opportunity of meeting the Deputy Inspector General of Police, Gordon,[130] who is likely to succeed Farmer as I.G. of Police. I also met the new District Judge, Bivar (accent on the second syllable), and I like the look of him. He's fairly senior in the Service, and I think his father and grandfather were civilians before him. He's the first European Sessions Judge at Faridpur for a dozen years, and he'll pull things together a bit.

I'm writing this in the cabin of the 'Rosalind'. We shall be reaching M'pur again in less than an hour. I hope to find the river has receded in the last two days. I took some photographs of my house surrounded by water, & I hope they'll be a success.

Madaripur, East Bengal
20 September 1937

I'm afraid that I've missed the Saturday mail this week because I've been so rushed off my feet that I've not had a moment to do anything except work. I've had to resort to Sherlock Holmes during mealtimes, which is a sure sign of overwork! However, I've escaped in the 'Rosalind' for a short breathing-space.

I've got heaps of your letters to answer, as you've taken to writing separately. . . .

The reason for my great pressure of work during the last few days is that I was on tour solidly from the 12th till the 16th, & so had an accumulation of urgent work and callers when I returned. It was a very strenuous tour, much of it in the real 'hinterland' in a country-boat.[131] This is the best time of year for such touring, as there is 'water, water everywhere'. Fortunately, I was favoured with fine weather all the time. I took quite a lot of photographs. My last film was on the whole successful, & I'll send you some prints soon. Really, the Bengal countryside has got a beauty of its own at this time of year. The abundant trees, fringing the rivers and streams, and the brilliant green of the paddy-fields are very pleasing to the eye.

We had our Union Board Subdivisional Conference yesterday. It was well-attended and everything went off well. I felt it was a great contrast from last year's show, when I knew so few of the Union Board Presidents & so little of their work. I'm beginning to feel quite an 'old stager' here now!

I shall be frantically busy till the 7th October, when the Puja holidays begin. Hill is touring in the subdivision again for 3 days at the end of the month, there's the District Board meeting on the 29th, and a hundred-&-one other things. I shall stay here during the Pujas, & let the other officers have their turn of a holiday. I may possibly be able to manage a week-end at Calcutta. Of course, the news about the Political *may* come in the first week of October. I shall quite enjoy a few days peace & quiet at Madaripur.

as from Madaripur, East Bengal
30 September 1937

My letters are being sent, I am afraid, at rather erratic intervals, but I have to seize what opportunities of leisure I can. I am writing today from Faridpur, where I have come once again for a District Board meeting. As Hafizuddin has not come this trip, I've had to come by Company steamer, instead of the launch. But at this time of year that is not inconvenient, and provides me incidentally with the luxury of a full-length bath![132]

I've been seeing a lot of Hill lately, as just before this trip, he was touring for 3 days in the subdivision. On the 25th, he distributed prizes at an Agricultural Exhibition at Haturia, the centre of the Tagore estate.[133] The next day we went on to visit a Physical Training Camp, which has been running for a fortnight at Kartikpur, under the guidance of a captain who is the Military Intelligence Officer. This is a new experiment, and seemed to be running quite well – about 70 schoolmasters and students all learning how to play games!

On the 27th, Hill divided his time between finishing off his inspection of my office, and presiding over a prize-distribution at Charmugria High School.

This month I shall have been away from headquarters no less than 18 days, so the short times I have been at Madaripur have been very busy indeed. I *still* haven't had time to finish Sir Edward Blunt's book on the I.C.S. However, in another week, I shall have rest during the Puja holidays. I may take a short week-end in Calcutta, but I'm not quite sure yet. It will be sufficiently pleasant simply to lead a leisurely life, getting up at 7.0 instead of 6.0, having meals at normal times, reading and writing letters, taking exercise daily, and sleeping a lot – oh, I forgot, playing the gramophone and gardening.

Mother has been pouring forth such a spate of letters recently that I hardly know how to answer them. ... To answer one or two miscellaneous questions; I get no time for reading at all, except at mealtimes, and light literature is then preferable. My staple drinks, except in the cold weather, are lemon squash & lime juice. Beer is much too heavy & soporific, and needs to be iced. I haven't formed the habit of a daily 'peg' of whisky-and-soda, but I have an occasional short drink before dinner to cheer me up – sherry, or gin-and-vermouth. . . .

[At this point, a letter is missing. My diary throws some light. I had been on tour on October 4th and 5th, with a streaming cold, to hear a 'Bad Livelihood' case, and on October 6th I was reduced to staying in bed all day. The entries for the next two days may speak for themselves – and incidentally reveal what a dull, factual record my diary was:

October 7. Completely recovered, so I did a full day's work – 13½ hours. A big dak & several visitors in the morning. Much executive work prevented me taking up the general file till nearly 2. What with two Transfer Petitions and 2 s.144 orders I left court at 8 (having taken a tea interval). Basket work[134] after dinner.

October 8. At 7.0 the Nazir brought me the staggering news that one A. K. Ghosh was appointed as S.D.O. Madaripur, and the *Gazette* confirmed this an hour later.[135] But I am quite in the dark as to where or when I shall go. Govt. of India? Calcutta?. . .

The next day (October 9) was the first day of the Puja holidays, and I wrote home that afternoon. No doubt the letter contained some fairly forcible speculation about my future.]

Madaripur, East Bengal
16 October 1937

After a week of suspense, I have at last received a letter from Hogg. It is of such importance that I shall reproduce it verbatim:

Darjeeling, October 13

Dear Saumarez Smith,

Carritt is going on leave at the beginning of January 1938, and it has been decided that you should come into the Secretariat to under-study him with a view to your taking over the duties of Under Secretary on Carritt's departure. This of course means that you will not go to the Foreign & Political Department, and that you will be expected to stick to the post for 2 years or thereabouts. It is realised that you had the question of leave in your mind, but you were prepared to give up that idea if selected for the Foreign & Political Department. I presume you would adopt the same attitude in respect of this proposal for employment in Carritt's post.

Yours sincerely,
(Sd) G. P. Hogg

The first thing to say about this letter is that I have received no formal intimation from Simla that my application for the F & P has been rejected. When I saw Hogg at the end of July, I gathered that the Bengal Government wanted to dissuade me from leaving them, and I suspect that this may be a sort of bait to attract me. If my application for the F & P has been successful, the Bengal Government has no power to prevent me going, as the I.C.S. is an all-India service. So I have just despatched a telegram to Capt. Hailey[136] asking if my application has been definitely rejected or not.

Assuming, however, that my application has been rejected, I am faced with a very difficult choice. The last two sentences of Hogg's letter do not give a true picture of the situation. I explained in detail in my long letter to you at the end of July that my leave might have to be postponed till the autumn of 1938, but that is quite a different thing from the spring of 1940. On the other hand, it is a fundamental condition of our service that we cannot claim leave as of right.

Now for the pros and cons of the job. It is definitely one of the three 'plums' for the young civilian. If I do not take this opportunity, I shall never be given a similar chance. The Under Secretaryship of the Political and Appointment Department is an exceedingly responsible, important, and arduous post. It brings one in close contact with the Governor, the Ministers, and all the 'burra sahibs' of the I.C.S. One lives a civilized life in Calcutta and Darjeeling. On the other hand, one loses all contact with the people of Bengal, one does no touring, but sits in an office all day, immersed in files;[137] and it will be tantalizing to live in Calcutta, and yet to have nearly as much work as I have here, where there are no counter-attractions. Further, if I have to wait till the spring of 1940, or at best the autumn of 1939, before taking my first leave, it cuts me off from England irremediably. After a lapse of 5 years, all my friends will have forgotten me. . . .

I shall lapse into pen now; I wanted to keep a carbon copy of the first two pages. I don't know what is happening to Pringle or his job. I had been under the impression that Carritt was not going on leave till March 1938, and so never thought that my transfer could be with reference to that post. I shall write again on Tuesday, when I expect to have more news.

I hoped to be able to enclose some photographs with this letter, but have not yet received them from Calcutta.

The past week has been idle but dull. I have cleared off a certain amount of work, read miscellaneously, taken some exercise in the form of regular walks, played the gramophone a good deal, and the flute once. I have also written the usual Confidential Leaving Note[138] for the use of my successor, giving him my idea of the main problems and personalities of the subdivision. This was a pretty big job, and I'd written 32 foolscap pages before I'd finished. I've not been in a mood to write letters with my future so uncertain, though my English correspondence is hopelessly in arrear.

Madaripur, East Bengal
20 October 1937

I promised to write by the next air mail, but really I've got little more news. Capt. Hailey has not replied to my wire, so I am still just as much in the dark about the F & P as I was before. To make confusion worse confounded, three days after Hogg wrote his letter, of which I sent you a copy, Carritt wrote saying 'I am afraid it was a mistake to notify Ghosh's posting to Madaripur before we were in a position to tell where you were going. There is being a "general post" immediately after the Pujas this year in which you are involved, & I promise to let you know at once when your destination is finally settled – at present it is rather vague.' This letter is most mystifying, since Carritt is Hogg's subordinate, and Hogg said 'it has been *decided* that you should come in to the Secretariat'. If at the end of all these 'alarums and excursions' I am sent to another subdivision, I shall be absolutely furious; anything more idiotic and bad for the administration than to take me away from a subdivision which I know, & where (to the best of my knowledge) I am not doing too badly, and send me to a strange subdivision for four months, I cannot imagine. Really, it is very trying. This uncertainty has quite spoilt my Puja holidays, as I have neither been able to pack up my things, nor make arrangements for the future, nor write half the letters I meant to. Leisure in Madaripur is precious, and I have wasted half of it. Office reopens the day after tomorrow, and from that day I shall be caught up into a whirl of incessant activity until I leave.

... I hope I shall know my fate when next I write.

Madaripur, East Bengal
30 October 1937

No definite news yet, but the plot thickens. At long last I got a reply from Hailey, who had taken a few days' leave which explains the delay. His letter is confidential, so please don't pass it on. The main paragraph runs: 'So far as we are concerned we are anxious to take you in. The Bengal Govt., however, say that they are unable to spare you now that Kitchin, of your year, has been selected by Laithwaite & H.E. as A.P.S.V.' (which being interpeted means that the Viceroy and his Private Secretary, Mr. Laithwaite,[139] have chosen Kitchin to be Assistant Private Secretary to the Viceroy). 'There is in fact at the moment a bit of a dog fight in high quarters over your body and though we have hopes of being able to extract you in the end we cannot say anything at the moment. There is nothing you can do about it now except to lie low and say nothing, but I should be glad if you would let me know whether even if you accept the Political Under Secretaryship you are still anxious to come into the Department.' (I'm not in a position to reply to this yet.)

This was a bit of a thunderbolt. I'd had no idea that Kitchin had been even angling for this job. However, as he's a personal friend of Sir John Anderson and also knows Laithwaite well, that explains it. Drucquer, Kitchin and I have all been fighting to get out of Bengal, and Kitchin has won the fight! My suspicions about Hogg's letter were quite correct. It was really rather a dirty trick to conceal from me the fact that the F & P were wanting me.

Hot on the heels of Hailey's letter came a telegram: 'Please reply Hogg's letter of October 13th regarding your intentions of taking leave.' I sent you a copy of that letter, and if you refer to it, you will see that it apparently required no answer. When the Chief Secretary writes personally to a junior civilian and says 'it *has been decided* that you should come in to the Secretariat . . . I *presume* that you would adopt the same attitude (about leave) in respect of this proposal. . .' the junior civilian accepts it as an order, not as a question. I was very glad that Hailey's letter had come in the nick of time.

I had been out on tour that day – my farewell trip in the 'Rosalind' – and I had to write a reply there and then to catch the evening post. (This all happened on the *26th* October, the memorable anniversary.)[140] As I was supposed still to know nothing about the 'dog-fight in high quarters', the situation called for some skill in drafting. I wrote a longish letter, ending with the words 'If I am selected as Carritt's successor, I should apply for a year's leave in the autumn of 1939, and give up my previous application for leave from March to October 1938. If I am not selected as Carritt's successor, but sent to another subdivision, I shall stick to my previous application for leave next year.' This more or less forces their hands into giving me Carritt's job. They won't do anything so stupid as to send me to another subdivision for four months. And if they decide to keep me at Madaripur, & cancel Ghosh's posting, they know that the F & P cat will soon be out of the bag, in which case I would be in a position to raise Cain for being misled.

I am looking forward to having my suspense ended. As Ghosh's leave expires on the 4th November, the position must be settled before then. In yesterday's *Gazette*, I saw to my surprise that both Drucquer & Kitchin have taken leave from the Puja holidays till the Christmas holidays. Kitchin, I suppose, as a break before he goes to Delhi, and Drucquer, I believe, because he has got into hot water at Kalimpong.[141] Neither of them wrote to me – but then rivals don't communicate their plans to each other! It is a disadvantage of this place that I am cut off from hearing of the machinations of Government.

The last week has been a very busy one. I was on tour on Tuesday, and spent the whole of Wednesday paying out compensation money to the owners of the land which has been acquired for the new Subdivisional Headquarters.[142] I am getting sick of the perpetual questions about where & when I am going, especially as I have to bottle up the truth. (That partly explains why I'm pouring it all out to you.) I am beguiling myself at mealtimes by reading Sinclair Lewis's *Elmer Gantry*, a show-up of American Nonconformists.

as from Bengal United Service Club, Calcutta
6 November 1937

I have just left Madaripur, and am writing this letter on board the steamer which is taking me towards Calcutta, to join my job in the Secretariat.

Your letters cheered me. The news of Margaret's expected baby is splendid. It makes one redouble one's hopes that Ronald will get the Florence job. . . . particularly as it is now settled that I shall not be able to take leave as I expected. I know this is a very great disappointment to you, as it is to me, but I was much encouraged by the way in which you accepted the news, and urged me to take Carritt's job. It would have been the act of a fool to refuse.

I am so very sorry that I failed to write for Father's birthday, but I confess this transfer business had put it out of my mind. I remembered it on All Saints' Day itself. (It's too late to do anything about it now, but I'll remember my omission at Christmas.) I have seldom had a more harassing day. There had been a recrudescence of an old dispute between two sects of Mahommedans, about congregational prayer, and about 3000 illiterate cultivators had come into Madaripur, led by their respective champions. They wanted there to be a 'bahesh', or public argument, about this highly contentious matter, but this would certainly have led to rioting and bloodshed, and I prohibited it. A small meeting was held, at which general religious subjects were discussed, as a safety-valve. This was presided over by Latif, who, with his knowledge of Islamic Law, was of the utmost assistance. Meanwhile, a telegram came from my successor, Ghosh, saying he proposed joining on the next day but one (Wednesday). And I still didn't know definitely where I was going!

However, the next morning my doubts were finally set at rest, when letters from Hogg & Carritt came, telling me to join as soon as possible in Calcutta. Carritt's stupid letter of the 16th was written in ignorance of the fact that Hogg had already written to me.[143] Hogg's letter continued to conceal the truth about my F & P application, saying that 'in view of the fact that the local Govt. proposed to take you for training as understudy to Carritt, the F & P have not pursued the question of taking you in the F & P Dept.' A diplomatic lie!

The next day, Tuesday, was fortunately a holiday on account of the Kali Puja, so I was able to arrange a compromise with the leaders of the two Mahommedan parties, write a couple of judgements, and do a little packing. On Wednesday morning, Ghosh arrived. The last three days have been filled with farewell parties, writing testimonials, packing, selling my furniture, & some of my china, as it will be expensive and useless to take it to Calcutta and store it. I managed to make several quite good bargains.

I like the look of Ghosh. He was previously S.D.O. near Chittagong in a very undeveloped area,[144] and will find Madaripur a great contrast. I left Madaripur with mixed feelings. I can't say my sixteen months there have been exactly happy, but they have been intensely interesting.

Notes

[108] The Saturday Club, alias 'The Slap', was the most popular club in Calcutta for junior business men and officials. Though I describe it as a 'second home' for Douglas Henderson, I do not think that one could stay there; but the facilities for eating, drinking, swimming, dancing and other recreation were excellent.

[109] Mr. Blank did go on four months' home leave in the winter of 1937/8.

[110] Maurice Curtis and Michael Hirtzel were both in the shipping firm of Macneills. Maurice was the son of Sir George Curtis, K.C.S.I., I.C.S., and Michael the son of Sir Arthur Hirtzel, who had been Permanent Under-Secretary at the India Office from 1924 to 1930. They shared a flat in Raja Santosh Road, Alipore, in south-west Calcutta, with Hugh (now Sir Hugh) Mackay-Tallack. When he was on leave in the summer of 1938, I moved into the flat for six enjoyable months. Maurice was killed in the Western Desert.

[111] Gerald Curtis joined the I.C.S. in the Punjab in 1929 and moved to the Political Service three years later. After Independence, he farmed near Saffron Walden and became a leading member of Essex County Council.

[112] There were four classes on Indian railway trains, 1st, 2nd, Intermediate ('Inter') and 3rd. When journeying on duty, one was expected to travel 1st (and thus entitled to claim travelling allowance at 1st class rates).

[113] Christopher Robinson was Bishop of Lucknow from 1947 to 1962, and Bishop of Bombay from 1962 to 1970. He then returned to the Cambridge Brotherhood House in Delhi (which I revisited in January 1973).

[114] I little imagined at that time that I would be working in those Secretariat buildings, from 1940 to 1943, as an Under Secretary to the Governor-General, Lord Linlithgow.

[115] The photographs included the best I ever took, one of the Taj Mahal.

[116] The Cecil Hotel was certainly comfortable, but the following description of it in *Freedom at Midnight* by L. Collins and D. Lapierre, published in 1975, does not tally at all with my own memories. 'A hostelry whose hospitality was as lavish as anywhere in the world. Each evening at 8.15 a turbaned butler marched down its carpeted corridors tolling a dinner gong as though it was a P & O steamer. The guests, in black tie and evening dresses, came down to dine at tables covered with Irish linen, Mappin and Webb silverware, Doulton porcelain and German Bohemian crystal glasses for champagne, whiskey, wine, port and water at each place.' As Collins and Lapierre describe Simla as a 'miniature Sussex hamlet', I distrust their accuracy!

[117] Lord Linlithgow had taken over from Lord Willingdon as Viceroy and Governor-General the previous year. Because of the war, his normal five-year term was extended by two years, till 1943.

[118] J. H. S. Shattock, C.M.G., O.B.E. joined the I.C.S. in Bengal in 1931. In 1937 he was an Under Secretary in the Defence Department of the Government of India. After Independence he joined the Diplomatic Service.

[119] Leslie R. Chambers had joined the I.C.S. in Bengal a year before me, but had been

ill when his settlement training was due. So he did it with the men a year junior to him, and I got to know him well. The friendship forged then still continues.

[120] Sir Gilbert P. Hogg, K.C.I.E., C.S.I. joined the I.C.S. in Bengal in 1908, and became Chief Secretary – the senior post in the Secretariat – in 1933.

[121] I had met Hector Wilkinson with the Millers when I had first arrived in Bengal. He had taken over as Commissioner of Dacca Division from Mr. Nelson (see Note 36) in May 1937.

[122] Babu Gurudas Banerji had not recovered from his pleurisy. His replacement, Babu Priya Nath Sarcar, was efficient but not quite so likeable.

[123] He had some reason to be conceited, since he was near the end of a successful judicial career having been a member of the Bengal Judicial Service, of which not many members attained the distinction of promotion to the post of District and Sessions Judge.

[124] This was very uncharacteristic of the Circle Officer, Sibchar, Babu Pyari Mohan Mukherji. He had a remarkable command of idiomatic English, and used to write most admirable and entertaining tour diaries and confidential reports.

[125] 'Ganja' is the now familiar cannabis or 'pot'.

[126] J. M. Bottomley, C.I.E. had joined the Indian Educational Service in 1911, and had become Director of Public Instruction (the seniormost post) by 1931.

[127] See Letter of 15 August 1936.

[128] J. C. Farmer, C.I.E. had joined the Indian Police in Bengal in 1906, and had become Inspector-General in 1935.

[129] Lord Brabourne was Governor of Bombay, and had been appointed to succeed Sir John Anderson as Governor of Bengal. He was himself being succeeded by Sir Roger Lumley (later Lord Scarbrough). The Brabournes' home in East Kent was less than twenty miles from Waldershare.

When, four months later, I became Under Secretary, Home Department, one side of my work was the arrangement of Durbars and other ceremonial functions, and this brought me in touch with Lord Brabourne. He was a wonderful person, and it was both a privilege and a pleasure to work for him. His sudden death in February 1939 was a tragedy for Bengal and for India.

[130] Sir A. D. Gordon, C.I.E. had joined the Indian Police in Bengal in 1907 and succeeded Mr. Farmer as Inspector-General in 1938. There were six Deputy Inspectors-General, five in charge of 'Ranges', corresponding to the five Commissioners' Divisions, and the sixth in charge of the C.I.D.

[131] Climatically, September was the least pleasant month of the year, as the sun was still very powerful, the rains were ending, and the humidity was at its maximum. Reference to my diary shows that this tour really deserved the adjective 'strenuous'. In addition to the usual work with Union Boards and schools, Debt Settlement Boards were being established all over the place, in an endeavour to lighten the monstrous load of debt which weighed down the average villager; and these had to be inspected. Other activities in this five-day tour included inspecting stud bulls imported from the Punjab to improve the local breed of cattle; collecting money for a new dispensary; and enquiring into the acquisition of a brickfield for the new subdivisional headquarters. And on return to the *Rosalind* in the evening, official correspondence had to be tackled. Yet I do remember positively enjoying that tour; 'experientia docet'.

[132] In my Madaripur bungalow I used a hip-bath. Before dinner, the 'pani-wallah' would put in the bathroom a couple of disused kerosene tins full of hot water; and the bearer would announce 'Ghusul taiyar hai' (Bath is ready!). Contrary to Maugham-like legends, I would *not* don evening dress for my solitary meal, but put on a pair of white drill trousers and a tennis-shirt.

[133] Haturia was in the extreme south-eastern corner of the subdivision. This estate was only a small part of the landed property of the Tagore family.

[134] 'Basket work' did not mean that I had taken to that handicraft as a recreational contrast to my intellectual activity. No, my orderly would fill a wickerwork in-tray on my desk with files, and I would labour away at them until they were finished or until sleep overcame me.

[135] The Nazir, Babu Chuni Lal Mukerjee, was the clerk in charge of all the practical business of seeing that the office was smoothly run. A. K. Ghosh was a couple of years senior to me in the I.C.S. The *Gazette* was the official *Calcutta Gazette*, printed weekly, containing all Government notifications.

[136] Captain Hailey had joined the Indian Political Service from the Indian Army, and was the Under Secretary, Foreign and Political Department. I must have met him in Simla, but he is not mentioned in the Letter of 22 July 1937.

[137] I wrote more truly than I knew. During the remaining ten years of my service in India, until Independence Day in August 1947, I had only eight months in district (work (as District Magistrate and Collector of Malda in North Bengal in 1943/4). All the rest of the time I was a Secretariat-wallah in Calcutta/Darjeeling and Delhi/Simla, 'immersed in files'.

[138] There was a very strong and valuable tradition of giving as much help as possible to one's successor when handing over charge of any post; if possible, overlap for a day or two was arranged. In any case, the Confidential Leaving Note would warn him of pitfalls to be avoided.

[139] Sir Gilbert Laithwaite, G.C.M.G., K.C.B., K.C.I.E., C.S.I. At the time of writing, he was Mr. J. G. Laithwaite, C.I.E., having become Lord Linlithgow's Private Secretary the previous year. He was extremely kind to my wife and myself when we were in Delhi from 1940 to 1943 – and indeed to all junior civilians. He was famous for his curry lunches.

[140] I had sailed from Southampton on 26 October 1934.

[141] Kalimpong was one of the two outlying subdivisions of Darjeeling district, both of which were usually filled by married junior civilians. Seth Drucquer was lucky to have been posted there, being unmarried.

[142] My diary records 'Paid out Rs. 15,000/- between 11.0 and 6.0, with a discrepancy of only Rs. 5/- at the end.' See also Envoi.

[143] Though Michael Carritt showed some inefficiency both over this appointment and in the Mysore business (see end of Letter of 14 February 1937), he ran the appointments side of his work very well in general, as I found when I took over charge from him. On the political side, however, see Note 74.

[144] Ajoy Ghosh had been S.D.O., Cox's Bazar, in 1935/6. This lay on the Bay of Bengal, sixty miles south of Chittagong, near the Burmese border and the Arakan coast.

3

Envoi

Two matters, one public and one personal, in the early nineteen seventies combined to rouse in me a great wish to revisit the Indian sub-continent before I became too elderly, and while there were still people whom I remembered and who remembered me. The public matter was the civil war in East Pakistan and the birth of Bangladesh. The personal one was that our second son, Richard,* after graduating at King's, Cambridge, had taken an M.Litt. degree at Delhi University, and had returned to Delhi in 1972 to do a Ph.D. under the aegis of King's.

In January 1973 the Archbishops of Canterbury and York gave me leave of absence for three weeks. I spent the time in the three places where I had worked as a young man – a week in Delhi, a week in Calcutta, and a week in Bangladesh. Because I had spent the whole of the intervening years since Independence Day in Church administration, my links with the Church in India and Bangladesh had become stronger than those with the State. (But I had a most interesting encounter in Government House, Calcutta – where I had worked in 1946/7 – with the Governor of West Bengal, Mr. A. L. Dias, who was a Bombay Civilian of my own year.) My hosts in Bangladesh were the Bishop of Dacca and the Oxford Mission Fathers at Barisal.

I had totally lost touch with Hafizuddin. He had stayed with us near Salisbury in 1950 when he was visiting England on a Police Staff Training Course, but there had then been a gap of more than twenty years, and – particularly after the Civil War – I did not know whether he was alive or dead. On the day I arrived in Dacca I consulted the telephone directory and to my delight found the entry 'A. K. M. Hafizuddin'. I rang him up and he recognized my voice immediately. The following day, he and his wife gave me tea. He had had a remarkable career – Inspector-General, East Pakistan; Chairman, East Pakistan Industrial Development Corporation;

* Richard was born in Darjeeling in 1945. Our eldest son, John, had been born in Simla in 1943.

and Pakistan Ambassador to Switzerland, Malta and the Vatican. So there were photographs in the sitting-room of Hafizuddin with the Queen in Malta, and with the Pope in Rome! (At the moment of writing, he is a member of the Bangladesh President's Council of Advisers, in charge of the Ministry of Industries, having been recalled from retirement.) I also met his elder daughter – whose 'Khir Khilai' I had attended in September 1936 (see Letter of 4 October 1936) – and son-in-law, Mr. Khaleque, who was Inspector-General of Police, Bangladesh.

On my last evening in Dacca the Hafizuddins gave the Bishop and me a splendid dinner (including that delicious fish, hilsa). The guests included Mr. and Mrs. Shams-ud-Doha; reference to him as the Superintendent of Police, Faridpur, are frequent in the letters. He had become a great-grandfather, but was full of vigour and talk, about his world-wide tours with the Food and Agriculture Organization of the United Nations, the introduction of a new type of spring paddy ('iri'), and his work with the Dacca Improvement Trust. Altogether, it was a most pleasant and nostalgic evening.

Meanwhile, I had spent a few days at the Oxford Mission in Barisal. For the return journey, the Bishop had most kindly made available his Land Rover and driver, Christopher Bala. The route from Barisal to Dacca lay directly through Madaripur. And so it came about that I revisited a place of which I had so many vivid memories, but on which I had never imagined I would set eyes again.

That it was possible to go by Land Rover from Barisal to Dacca at all showed the progress in road communication. There was one long steamer trip of two and a half hours, and several short ferries – some bridges broken during the Civil War had not yet been repaired – but for most of the distance it was straightforward driving on reasonable roads. Of course, it was the cold weather; but it will be recalled that in December 1936, it had taken me twenty-four hours' extremely circuitous journeying to get from Faridpur to Madaripur, a direct distance of less than forty miles.

The first thing that greeted my eyes at the 'new' subdivisional headquarters at Sakuni was a really splendid large tank. I was welcomed by several clerks in the S.D.O.'s office, situated on the banks of the tank; the S.D.O. himself had gone to Rajair for a meeting with the Food Minister. On the office desk I saw to my astonishment a *telephone*! Such a thing was undreamt of in my time. On the wall, as if to convince me that I was not in a Rip Van Winkle dream, was a list of S.D.O.s. The present incumbent was No. 44 on the list, and I was No. 8, with Susil Dey No. 7 and Ajay Ghosh No. 9. At this moment the Second Officer, Maulvi Razzaque Majumdar, arrived. It was the great festival of Bakr-Id, so the office was closed, but I was driven round to see the hospital. Then we went on to Charmugria, and there met the Grand Old Man of Madaripur, a much respected doctor, Rai Sahib K. C. Saha. (Incidentally, Mr. Majumdar had saved the Rai Sahib's life during the Civil War.) The Rai Sahib remembered me, and we gossiped of the days gone by.

Returning to Madaripur, I had an hour's rest in the extremely comfortable and well-equipped Inspection Bungalow. (It even boasted a flush loo, which was a marked advance from the regime of commodes and sweepers thirty-six years previously.) It was then time for an excellent lunch, which was laid on by Maulvi Syed Abdul Majid, a retired pleader aged seventy-two, who reminded me that he had helped me with the land acquisition proceedings at Sakuni – see Letter of 30 October 1937. Considering that my visit was totally unheralded, this was a truly remarkable example of spontaneous hospitality. Immediately after lunch, Christopher Bala drove me on to Faridpur, giving a lift to Mr. Majumdar as far as Rajair. We stayed overnight at a Baptist Mission. I tried to contact the District Magistrate (now styled Deputy Commissioner); but he was unfortunately away for the day. I slept that night without a mosquito-net – yet another example of progress.

In fact I did not sleep well, for my mind was too full of memories.

Appendix A

Addresses of welcome were frequently presented to visiting officials. The language of this one is absurdly amusing; but it illustrates forcibly the defects of the educational system. It is to be remembered to the Headmaster's credit that he was doing his best in 'a charland inhabited by many uneducated souls'.

TO.

K. A. L. Hill. M.A. (Cantab) Esqr, I.C.S.,

District Magistrate & Collector, Faridpur.

THE SALT OF FARIDPUR.

"A type of the wise who soars but never roams
True to the kindred point of heaven and home".
Paxvobiscum! Paxvobiscum! Paxvobiscum!

May it please your Honour,

Heavy is our heart with grief, neutralised are our limbs, dim are our eyes—our most leaf-and-dear, revered King Emperor George V has given up his ghost. He has gone to a land undiscovered from whose bourne no traveller turns up. But darkness can not reign for good.— "Old order changeth, yielding place to new". Just behold, when one Sun sets, another sun, with full eradiation of renewed glory makes his appearance, giving birth to a new era of peace, comfort & prosperity. Under this shadow of a great bereavement but at the same time in the sunshiny splendour of a glorious installation, we, the teachers of Sakhipura Islamia H. E. School, with one eye full of tears & the other beaming with happy simpering, consider it to be a proud privilege to accord you, —representative of our King,—a most cordial reception of greeting.

Wel-comed, wel-comed are you, august & up to snuff. Gramercy, gramercy! my revered father, for thy undergoing the legitimate trouble of trying to grow the seed of felicity in us. Perfect is your soul. You have the mind pregnant with celestial feeling dawning to our life-dawn. Among men of letters with ripe and judicious Judgment specially eulogised you are; effulgence of lore is your vestment; you have known how well to appreciate the *tokalon* of education.

Bengal has been passing through a phase of great political unrest for the last few years. We have been silted up. We have been translated into cypher, we have been rendered into nothingness; we have been manikin. Bereft of commonsense we have been; monocephalous & profligate we have been. Terrorism has been, as it were, our constant companion. We think it to be a task most trying to eradicate this evil from within us,—evil which has shaped us what we are. To try to do away with the germs throws light on the breach of principle on which our nature dogmatic in cognito is based. The baneful and pungent consequence of this is a frequence, tending to station us gradually with a more grotesque aspect in such an awkward juncture of life that it has been an impossibility to keep the wolf from the door by seeing us to pay debt to nature, unhonoured and unsung.

Demoralizing and life-killing as this activity of anarchism has been, we have always tried our best to get it, exotic as it is in the sacred land of many a soul, making an uncommon noise in the face of the universe by reaching the pinnacle of glory, weeded out of existence, in co-operation with the Government. We have rendered an humble mite but we know not how far our legitimate effort in the matter has been fruitful in success. We have been trying our best to give a developed nourishment to the eradication of this terrible monster, Terrorism. But it is cock-sure,—nay we can, by the name of God and with heart within, asure you, Sir, that we will never flag in our determination to kill entirely this evil of terrorism from the holy land until, and unless we are assured of its safe burial deep beneath the earth, never to pop up its ugly head again. Now let us be filled with the spirit of pure enthusiasm. Let us be up and doing. Let us be actuated by the feeling of loyalty. Let us be enthusiastically putting our shoulder to the wheel with one shoulder—wheel that is attended with the holy velocity of speed prognosticating the future prolific in closely legitimate touch with the Government.

You are erudite with high worth tangible. You are typically loyal. You are fully aware of the significance of your gravely responsible task incumbent on you. You have been trying your utmost with auspicious consequence to see your subjects free from indulging in Terrorism and *otherisms*.

Sakhipura is a charland inhabited by many uneducated souls. It is enveloped in the mist of ignorance. It is deprived of enjoying the beauty and bliss of life in to-to. The new birth of the Sakhipura Islamia H. E. school has been, for the last 7-8 years, trying to drive this darkness to some extent by giving birth to some educated boys who, if provided by the Government, will be a sure guarantee for the attraction of the public towards their obtaining education with full jocundity. But it is a matter of deep regret that the school, owing to the fact of its not being well-fed, is going to reach a decaying plight. It has to depend entirely on income meagre and sources fungus. That the existence of the Institute is a great necessity is an admitted fact hinging on future improvement of the place. This being so, we invite your kind and sympathetic attention to the fact of your kindly taking our cause of your redressing the impediments and inconvenience it has been labouring under as a consequence of the absence of good roads, tube-wells, a charitable dispensary, a post office here. We hope you will be kind enough to have the long-felt desiderate removed, so that the school may be financially improved with the bliss of permanent recognision.

Sir, it will, I think, be a permanent source of income to the school if you kindly so arrange as 6 pies per Rupee may be collected from each Khashmohal tenant in addition to what is paid by each tenant.

My thanks are due to the officials, the gentle, and the gentry present here.

Sir,

With low conge we regret to add eventually that we have nothing to pay as a token of respect to you, our *summumbonum* for your kind and auspicious trouble you have undergone for presiding over this function with a happy view of seeing peace perfect reigning over your Sakhipur jurisidiction. However, this yields some amount of satisfaction of gratitude that we have not been shilly-shallying to show our deep obeisance to the Government in strict harmony with your call, after going on through the path of duty—'Be obedient, where obedience is due'—with the evil germ of terrorism being stamped out of existence from within us: this has acted, acts and will act as wholesome stimulas to enable us to be loyal to the British Crown, truthful, dutiful and enriched fully, come what may.

May God grant you a long and happy life of administration. Sincerely wishing you thorough success in life untrammelled and unhampered by any insurgency of political cataclysm and offering you at the same time our right hand of assistance and co-operation whenever and under whatever circumstances such aid and co-operation may stand necessary.

Dated, Sakhipura,
The 7th October, 1936.

We have the honour to be, Sir
Your most obedient servants
Suresh Chandra Banerjee B. A. Rector
Sakhipura H. E. School &
The Teaching Staff

Appendix B

Glossary of words not explained in text or notes
(In order of appearance)

MOFUSSIL	The opposite to 'headquarters'. When in Calcutta, the rest of Bengal was 'mofussil'; when in Faridpur, Madaripur was 'mofussil'; when in Madaripur, the rest of the subdivision was 'mofussil'.
SAIS	Groom.
DURZI	Tailor.
PANI-WALLAH	Scullion and general bottle-washer, at beck and call of both bearer and cook.
ZEMINDAR	Landowner.
BURRA SAHIB	Anybody holding a senior or important position ('burra' = big): hence, one's boss. I was a 'chota sahib' in Madaripur ('chota' = small), and Mr. Hill was my 'burra sahib'.
PICE	A coin worth about a farthing. Four pice made one anna, worth slightly more than a penny (old style). Sixteen annas made one rupee, worth one shilling and sixpence. There was an even smaller coin, the pie, worth one-third of a pice; it resembled, I recall, the current half-penny (new style).
SHIKAR	Huntin' and shootin'.
DAK	(pronounced 'dark'). Post. Dak-wallah = Postman.
SERANG	Boatswain.
PUJA	Hindu religious rites: hence, a Hindu festival holiday.
MUKHTEAR	Criminal court lawyer.
BANDABAST	Pronounced and sometimes spelt 'bundabust', and almost untranslatable, but 'arrangement' and 'preparation' are not far out. A 'pukka bandabast' was an efficient arrangement.
KHASHMOHAL	Government estate.

Index

† Indicates members of the Indian Civil Service.